Out to Change the World

Richard Armstrong

Out to Change the World

A Life of Father James Keller
of The Christophers

CROSSROAD · NEW YORK

1984
The Crossroad Publishing Company
370 Lexington Avenue, New York, N.Y. 10017

Library of Congress Cataloging in Publication Data
Armstrong, Richard, 1932–
Out to change the world.
Includes bibliographical references and index.
1. Keller, James, 1900–1977. 2. Catholic
Church—United States—Clergy—Biography.
3. Christophers (Organization) I. Title.
BX4705.K34A76 1984   267'.182'0924 [B] 84-9494
ISBN 0-8245-0651-0

Acknowledgment
"I Believe"—Words and Music by Ervin Drake, Irvin Graham,
Jimmy Shirl and Al Stillman. TRO—Copyright 1952 (renewed 1980)
and 1953 (renewed 1981) Hampshire House Publishing Corp., New York,
N.Y. Used by permission.

To all the Christophers, known and unknown,
who have proven by their lives
that it is possible to change the world.

Contents

Foreword

It was 1949, two months before my graduation from high school. My father came to my room while I was studying for an exam and put a red covered book on my desk. "I want you to read this," he said. "I think you'll like it." He was right. The book, *You Can Change the World*, by Father James Keller was like an electric shock.

I was seventeen years old, idealistic and floundering; wondering what career to follow, full of anxiety about the future. I wanted to do something meaningful with my life, but didn't know what. Father Keller's book came at just the right time. His clarity and optimism gave me a new confidence. There was a job for me to do in this world, a God-given mission. It was just a question of time before I would find it.

Father Keller motivated his readers to choose careers where they could do the most good: politics, education, communications; wherever they might put their talents to work to make this a better world. His thinking liberated me to pursue my ideals, and I began preparing for educational television.

Joan Ganz Cooney, the creator of "Sesame Street" and now president of the Children's Television Workshop, told me she, too, had been influenced by Father Keller, and after college entered the field of communications in the same idealistic spirit. Her impact on the industry is well known.

My television dreams, however, were short-lived. After college and some obligatory time in the military, I began to reevaluate my own goals. A strong desire for the priesthood was growing within me. I wanted a more direct and immediate way of becoming a

Christbearer. I abandoned the idea of a career in TV and entered the seminary.

Father Keller's influence on me continued throughout my seminary years. Little did I know at the time that one day I would carry on the important work he began. I didn't know anything about the struggle it took to make his dream come true. His life seemed to flow serenely, without complication. I saw him as one who was born to succeed as though by some magical predilection.

It was only after some years of working within the Church myself that I came to realize what a monumental task it was to effect even a modicum of change. As I learned more about the history of The Christophers, I gained a deeper understanding of James Keller's perseverance.

Many of his contemporaries misunderstood him and his dream; his determination seemed to rub them the wrong way. He often put business before personal considerations. He was both tough and very gentle, the same qualities I admire in Christ. In spite of the great support he received from thousands of admirers, he remained humble. In fact, he was embarrassed by praise. He inspired loyalty and devotion in his followers and coworkers without courting favor, and he was eminently practical.

James Keller was among the first in the Church to recognize the potential of the mass media for bringing Christ to vast audiences. Though he considered himself poor in the talents needed to succeed in radio and TV, others recognized that his good looks and clear thinking made him an appealing spokesman for the Gospel. His fidelity to daily prayer was well known and it surely sustained him through many trials. His singleness of purpose caused him to ask much of those around him, and much more of himself.

This book you are about to read is a monograph, a brief sketch of Father Keller's struggle to bring The Christophers to life. It is an honest book but in some ways less than complete. The story of his spirituality would take an entire book in itself.

Let me give you an example. During his final illness, which lasted a few years, he wrote the following spiritual testament. It gives an insight into the heart of the man:

August 14, 1972

Since tomorrow, August 15th, the Feast of the Assumption, is the 47th anniversary of my ordination, it seems to be a fitting time to ponder more seriously than ever before the fact that a relatively short time is left for me to prepare for my final summons.

Throughout my life I have looked forward with joyful anticipation to the "homecoming" day when I will meet my Savior face to face and hear Him say: "Come, blessed of My Father, possess you the kingdom prepared for you from the foundation of the world."

But the nearer I get to that glorious occasion, the more unworthy I feel. I find myself counting more than ever before on the mercy of the Lord to make up for my defects and shortcomings. I appreciate more and more what St. Paul must have meant when he said to the Romans: "We have all sinned and are deprived of the glory of God." (Rom. 3:23)

But willing and generous as God is to forgive all our faults, He decrees that we do some penance for our sins either here or in the next life.

From every point of view it seems much more sensible to do all the scrubbing and cleansing during our brief sojourn on earth rather than wait for it to be done in the hereafter.

Through prayer and good works during my short life span I can do penance for my imperfections and prove that I am truly sorry for any and all of my offenses against a loving God, e.g.,

—by increasing my prayers for the work of The Christophers, for numerous intentions involving the eternal salvation and human well-being of many friends and acquaintances, as well as the poor people of the earth;

—by accepting cheerfully the handicap of my physical ailments;

—by welcoming rather than evading any suffering that the Lord allows to come my way and to do this in honor of His passion and death on the Cross;

—by trying to be of greater service to mankind through working for The Christophers;

—by striving to bring joy, not gloom, into the lives of others;

—by avoiding all forms of self-pity;

—by fulfilling more devotedly all daily spiritual exercises;

—by endeavoring to be so conscientious about all my obligations as a priest that I may be under all circumstances a humble witness of the holiness, devotion, generosity, detachment and purity that most people associate with a good priest;

—by continually thanking God for the countless blessings I have received from Him throughout my life;

—by recalling frequently St. Paul's important reminder: "By God's favor you were saved. This is not your own doing, it is God's gift." (Eph. 2:8);

—by faithfully living up to the spiritual goal set by the prophet Micah: "This is what the Lord asks of you, only this—to act justly—to love tenderly—and to walk humbly with your God."

James Keller

Father Keller died a holy death on February 7, 1977. One Maryknoll priest who visited him often while he was dying said that Jim had no sense of having done anything particularly noteworthy in his life. He was humble to the very end. And now as the years pass and we gain some perspective on his life, we can understand more fully the greatness of his accomplishments. This after all is his legacy to all of us.

"By their fruits you will know them."

Father John Catoir
Director of The Christophers

Preface

Father James Keller, M.M. (1900–1977) was many things to many people: a media personality who seemed to be everywhere but who kept people at a cordial distance . . . a foreign missioner who never served overseas . . . an unpolished speaker who could light up an audience by his enthusiasm . . . a compulsive worker who tried to find time for everyone . . . the bearer of a revolutionary message who deferred to authority . . . a friend of the rich who often dined alone in cheap restaurants . . . a believer in God who helped people to believe in themselves.

The sixteen years during which I was Father Keller's close associate were exciting ones. It was exhilarating merely to be around him. His infectious laugh and playful manner were qualities one did not usually associate with a priest. There were always new projects: career guidance schools . . . the alleviation of world hunger . . . the spiritual foundations of American history . . . peaceful uses of the atom . . . dramatic films with established stars . . . leadership books and courses . . . the need for "good people" in politics, teaching, and every aspect of the communications media . . . a dynamic rewriting of the Baltimore Catechism . . . a conference to revitalize the training of future priests. No wonder his editorial assistants came and went. Few could keep up with this cheerful, slave-driving whirlwind of a man.

Contrary to what I had picked up via the clerical grapevine, Father Keller was neither aloof nor manipulative. He was sixty when I first met him, and the years may have mellowed any sharpness or impatience of his youth. I saw a gracefully aging man whose youthful impetuosity had been tempered by kindness and wisdom.

I saw a man who never missed reading the *New York Times* or the New Testament. He would reduce the newspaper to a pile of clippings and mark the Bible with underscoring. Both became part of his consciousness and often formed the basis for his latest project.

To those who worked with Father Keller in television, his patience was legendary. Script deadlines, hot lights, camera failures, tight shooting schedules—in the face of these, and more, he never complained. One time, the only thing that kept an overheated, overworked crew from walking off the job was the sight of the man in the black suit who accepted every discomfort without murmur.

Toward the end of an intensely active life, James Keller was forced to accept, not discomfort, but inaction and declining health. He had to practice the acceptance of adversity he had always preached. This he did with a serenity and good nature that deeply impressed those who were near him.

This book is neither a hagiography nor an exposé. If it accomplishes its purpose, it will awaken memories in those who knew Father Keller and provide an introduction to those who did not. This story of his life illustrates the message he never tired of repeating—and which the Christopher movement continues to proclaim. He believed in the uniqueness of the human person: "There's nobody like you." He believed in the power for good in each individual: "You can make a difference."

* * *

I wish to thank all those who permitted me to interview them in the preparation of this book. Special thanks are due to Father John Catoir, director of the Christophers, who allowed me to use the Christopher archives; and to Father John Halbert, M.M., who gave me access to the archives at Maryknoll. I am indebted to Donald Brophy, editor of Paulist Press, for his invaluable critique of my first draft. I am grateful to Dr. Edward Wakin, professor of communication at Fordham University, for his constant encouragement. I am most appreciative of the help given me by Mrs. Mildred Burns of Oakland, California, Father Keller's sister, who entrusted me with a treasured family album. Not least, I wish to express my gratitude to Mrs. Barbara Newington and Mr. David Smith, without whose help this labor of love would never have been completed.

Richard Armstrong

•1•

"Stay in Your Own Back Yard!"

"You will never bring out the bit of greatness within you, if you set your sights low."

James Keller

August 1935—Two men sat on the beach at the posh resort of Southampton on Long Island and gazed at the sea. They talked of many things, mainly the future plans of the younger man, a lawyer. As often as they had met, the older man, a priest, had repeated the theme that the law should be used for public service, not just for private gain. The younger man had listened. Nearly thirty-five years later, in 1969, he found himself at a negotiating table in Vienna, hammering out the first—and only—strategic arms limitation treaty between the U.S. and the U.S.S.R. Ambassador Gerard C. Smith never forgot those summer days on the beach when his friend, the priest, planted in his mind the seed that would grow into a lifetime career in public service.

* * *

June 1943—Two middle-aged men labored over a manuscript spread out on a large desk. One was a leading reporter for the *New York Times*, the other a priest. The reporter, a brilliant writer and a notorious procrastinator, was finally completing the book about young Americans who were risking their lives for the oppressed in the war-torn Orient and in the jungles of South America. The priest supplied the stories and good-naturedly goaded his fellow worker into getting down to business. Meyer Berger, who seven years later won a Pulitzer Prize for reporting, provided the essential ingredient of a superior writing style to the book which was to

I

become a best-seller, *Men of Maryknoll*. The priest, its coauthor, was beginning to learn the writing trade.

* * *

MAY DAY, 1947—Hundreds of thousands of Catholics and people of other faiths gathered for public prayers, rallies, and religious parades aimed at the peaceful conversion of Russia. In New York, Cleveland, Detroit, Cincinnati, Baltimore, Washington, and more than a hundred other major cities, crowds of up to 10,000 stood or knelt, often in the rain, giving a positive demonstration of faith on a day traditionally overshadowed by ceremonies under the red banner of Communism. At St. Patrick's Cathedral in New York, the priest who spearheaded the nationwide campaign addressed a crowd of 4,000, while another 6,500 waited outside. He called the demonstration a "lesson of Christian love on a supernatural basis that would leave a lasting impression on the general public and possibly the world."

* * *

AUGUST 1965—Two priests, one of them a Spanish Jesuit theologian, ate a hurried supper in the Dixie Kitchen cafeteria on 48th Street in New York City. They talked about the third Christopher Study Week, just concluded, which had brought together leading theological experts from all over the world to propose ways to implement the documents of the Second Vatican Council as they related to the training of future priests. The older man suddenly became reflective and said to Jose Calle, S.J.: "You know, Joe, that I am not a writer. I am not a good speaker. I am not a theologian. I am not even a good administrator. I can't boast of great experience in mission lands. As a matter of fact, I have very few talents. All I try to do is to put to good use the few gifts I have received from the Lord. But this is precisely the message that I want to convey through the Christopher idea—that everybody, even those with few talents like myself, can be an effective missionary."

* * *

SPRING 1948—After a quiet dinner in the Navarro Hotel in New York City, an anxious author gave the untitled manuscript of his book to his host, a *Reader's Digest* senior editor. Later that evening, Fulton Oursler, having scanned the pages with practiced skill, told the writer he had a title. On one of the pages, he had spotted the words, "you can change the world." He added, "That is the title for your book. I predict it will be a best-seller." It was.

* * *

FEBRUARY 1952—Two hundred leaders in the fields of motion pictures, newspapers, magazines, books, radio, and television attended a dinner at the Crystal Room in the Beverly Hills Hotel for the third annual presentation of the Christopher Awards. Prize money amounting to $25,000 was awarded to fourteen persons whose creative work demonstrated the far-reaching good that could be accomplished by one individual. Comedian Jimmy Durante provided musical entertainment for the presentation, which was broadcast over the NBC radio network. In his introductory remarks, the priest who had originated the awards stated: "It cannot be emphasized too strongly that 8,000 Christopher friends over the country have made these awards possible. . . . Each dollar is a vote of confidence on the part of some individual that those in the creative fields can present to the public the high quality entertainment and literary works they really want and deserve. This gift is one more proof of the great good that little people can do."

* * *

JUNE 1969—An aging priest in deteriorating health lay down for his noontime nap on a couch in his second-floor office in midtown New York. He was officially retired, the result of the onset of Parkinson's disease. The next day, June 27, would be his sixty-ninth birthday. By prearranged signal, a Christopher staff member awoke him and led him to an elevator, which took them to a first-floor auditorium. A door opened. Father James Keller, founder and, for twenty-four years, director of the Christophers, stepped unsteadily through the entrance to hear a throng of employees and friends warmly cry, "Happy Birthday!"

For the next hour, amid the laughter of friends, he sat in the front row watching a homemade production of "This Is Your Life, James Keller," with words and music written for the occasion.

The opening number, based on an autobiographical account of his childhood in Oakland, California, echoed the words of his harried mother (to the tune of "Stay in Your Own Back Yard"):

> *You'll catch your pants on a nail*
> *If you climb that rail!*

Stay in your own back yard.
Just stay this side of the fence.
Please don't be dense.
Stay in your own back yard.
Oh, you can go to the East
Go to the West,
But you're sure to get
Trouble galore, you ain't seen nothin' yet!
Don't light a candle, my dear!
Just stay right here,
Safe in your own back yard!

As the affectionate parody of his life unrolled, Keller laughed with amusement and pleasure. The man who had given Christopher Awards to hundreds of the country's leading producers, directors, and writers was utterly surprised. He had never expected this sort of outpouring for himself.

The "back yard" song particularly delighted Keller. It reminded him of the days of his childhood when, eager for excitement, he wandered off in search of adventure. Oakland in the early 1900s was a city of private homes, with high wooden fences circumscribing their back yards. It was in his own back yard that Keller's mother wanted him to stay "like a good little boy." If being good meant staying at home, Keller would have none of it. He would find another way. From the very start, he wanted to see the world. Later he would want to change it.

It was not that Keller's parents had always been stay-at-homes. His father, James Kelleher, had left his native Ireland in 1885 at the age of eighteen to join an uncle who had preceded him to Oakland. On November 19, 1890, he married Margaret Selby, whose family had settled in Chicago before coming west. By the time of his marriage, Kelleher had shortened his name to Keller, as his uncle had done before him. The reason may have been to allay existing prejudices against the Irish, or it may have been an accommodation to WASP, or "Anglo," sensibilities. If so, it was an indication that the future priest would attempt to avoid any hint of "foreignness" in his dealings with individuals or in his presentation of his Church's teachings.

James and Margaret Keller had six children between 1890 and 1905: Hazel, Harold (who died of tuberculosis in his early twenties), Louis, James (1900), Reginald, and Mildred.

James, Sr., was a large man with a solid frame that might have made him appear intimidating if it had not been for his soft-spoken manner. He had a strong temper, but rarely displayed it. A devout man, he would lead his entire household to 8:00 A.M. Mass each Sunday at St. Francis de Sales Church in Oakland. After Mass came breakfast at Grandmother Selby's, a prosperous business-woman who owned a number of private homes in Oakland. James, Sr., had gone into the haberdashery business, but despite hard work he had no flair for business. The Selbys were far better at this than the Kellers. Young James probably picked up his penchant for advertising, public relations, and marketing from his mother's side of the family.

The highlight of the week for the Keller children was the Sunday afternoon walk with their father. Despite his reticent manner and occasional outbursts of (usually justified) anger, he was a soft-hearted man who habitually carried a bag of mints in his pocket to secretly slip to each of his children in turn. The favored child, thinking himself or herself the sole recipient of this good fortune, felt singled out as the object of special affection.

Margaret Selby Keller was a rotund woman, Irish on her mother's side and Portuguese on her father's. Like many mothers, she worked small miracles with little ready cash, always seeing to it that her children were well fed and well dressed. Keeping up appearances with better-off neighbors was important to her, but more important was the affection she had for them. Margaret was more demonstrative toward her children than was her husband, and was also somewhat overprotective of them.

Among all his brothers and sisters, the young James was closest to Louis, who was a year older than himself. The pair shared an upstairs bedroom in the family's two-story frame house at 16th and West streets in Oakland. As they grew older, however, their interests diverged. Louis never went to college, but became a plumber's apprentice and eventually started his own contracting business. In later years, Louis, the self-made man with the rough manner, would refer to James as "my stuffy brother"—a not altogether complimentary nod to the fact that James could be described as "genteel"—that the company of wealthy and well-educated people appealed to him.

Hazel was the oldest child in the Keller household. She was her mother's surrogate and had the older sister's penchant for dominating as well as caring for her younger siblings. She stayed at home with her parents until, at the age of forty, she married Thomas McCabe. A scrapbook she lovingly kept for years about the activities of James has provided much information on his life not otherwise obtainable.

Reg Keller seems to have been the hellion of the family and as a boy was usually the object of his father's occasional outbursts. Later he attended the University of California at Los Angeles where he made contacts that served him well, both as a Cadillac salesman in the 1930s and later in the real estate business in southern California. Reg had Lou's gruff manner and James' educational opportunities, and often told his priest-brother how to do his job, whether for Maryknoll or the Christophers—advice to which James did not always take kindly. During a visit to Reg's family at their Lake Tahoe vacation spot one day in 1945, James sat silently at the dinner table while his younger brother told him that he was going about the launching of the Christophers all wrong. Unable to take it any longer, James stood up and declared: "I'm not the dummy you think I am." With that, he turned and left the room. Though the two brothers were never close, Reg did occasionally help find potential supporters for Christopher projects.

Mildred, the youngest of the Keller children, was like James in many ways and was his favorite. Her gentleness and even shyness covered a strong sense of determination. In the early 1940s, James helped Mildred get a job in New York City, evidently hoping that the move would broaden her horizons. Not long afterward, he found her a secretarial position at the Newman School in Lakewood, New Jersey, a Catholic prep school, where she met Joseph Burns, a teacher at the school. The two were married and eventually returned to the Bay area, where Joseph worked for Lou Keller's contracting firm.

Once he left home at the age of twenty-one to become a missioner, James effectively said good-bye to his family. He dutifully visited his relatives, but he was usually on the run. Even in his mother's home, he frequently spent more time on the telephone than talking with family members. The paradox of Keller's life is that this man, who taught love so effectively to millions, could not quite find the way to share himself with his own family or, later, with the priests with whom he lived. His commitment to his work—God's work, as he saw it—was so complete that he had little time or inclination to enjoy the pleasures of home and of intimate friendships that most people value so highly.

Even as a child, Keller possessed a more than ordinary interest in the things of God. When it came time for him to choose a career, it is not surprising that he felt called to the priesthood. What is surprising is that, through a variety of circumstances he regarded as providential, he was drawn to a missionary vocation that promised to lead him to the "farthest ends of the earth."

•2•

The Seed

"And gradually I began to realize that, when all was said and done, my vocation in life was to be a priest."

James Keller

SPRING 1910—St. Francis de Sales Church, Oakland, California. A parish priest was conducting a religious instruction class for a group of public school students preparing for First Holy Communion. Almost as an aside he said, "One of you kids may become a priest someday and do some good for the world." A ten-year-old, thinking the words were directed at him, ducked under a desk, hoping that it wasn't so. *A seed was planted.*

* * *

SPRING 1912—A new curate at St. Francis de Sales called aside an altar boy who had been serving his Mass and asked him: "Have you ever thought of becoming a priest?" The youth of twelve responded with a nod of his head, then wondered where the answer came from. *The seed was nurtured.*

* * *

SUMMER 1914—A conversation on the front porch of a large frame house between a priest and a middle-aged couple. "Your son has a vocation," the priest announced. The mother expressed surprise. The father was disappointed, sensing the loss of a helper in business. Nevertheless, with a reluctance mixed with pride the parents agreed that their son might indeed desire to be a priest. *The seed was taking root.*

* * *

FALL 1917—A youthful seminarian returned to St. Patrick's Minor (high school) Seminary in Menlo Park, California. He was troubled,

8

assailed by doubts over whether he should continue. His summer work at a resort in the Yosemite Valley had exposed him to a world that both attracted and repelled him. He was filled with distaste for the language and behavior of his companions. But the freedom of the outdoors and his easy conversations with park visitors drew him out of himself, making the seminary seem sterile and confining. *The seed was dormant.*

* * *

CHRISTMAS 1917—Albert and Walter Selby offered their nephew, fresh out of the seminary, a position as assistant manager of their large candy factory and soda fountain. He accepted. *The seed was choked by thorns.*

* * *

SPRING 1918—A young man nearly eighteen entered a U.S. Army recruiting station in San Francisco, hoping to take part in World War I. His application was rejected because the war was all but over. *The seed was practically forgotten.*

* * *

SPRING 1918—A man in a black suit and white Roman collar sat at the counter of a soda fountain in San Francisco and ordered a sundae. The young man who served him quickly engaged him in earnest conversation. Feeling pressured by the youth to agree with his declared intention not to reenter the seminary, the priest refused to discourage what might be a call from God. *The seed began to reemerge.*

* * *

SEPTEMBER 1918—A tall, slim youth with broad shoulders methodically packed a suitcase in preparation for a second try at seminary life. A summer of "hitting the books" enabled him to pass an examination that permitted him to rejoin his classmates. Soon afterward, he would hear the joyous news that, owing to a clergy shortage brought on by the war, his entire class would be advanced one year closer to ordination. *The seed deepened its roots.*

* * *

FALL 1918—A hushed group of seminarians at St. Patrick's, Menlo Park, California, listened attentively as the leader of the first American Catholic missionary group to go overseas described his plans for the conversion of China. One seminarian in particular came away with the impression that his calling might lie far beyond the confines of the Bay area of San Francisco. A wider world was making its appeal felt once more, only this time a world in need of healing. *The seed grew into a healthy stalk.*

* * *

"The kingdom of heaven is like a mustard seed which a man took and sowed in his field. It is the smallest of all seeds, but when it has grown it is the biggest shrub of all and becomes a tree so that the birds of the air come and shelter in its branches."

Matthew 13:31

* * *

Seminarian Keller was deeply impressed that four priests, three of them not much older than himself, had chosen to go into exile to proclaim the Gospel. The leader of the missionary group was Father Thomas F. Price, fifty-nine, a veteran missioner in his native North Carolina.[1] Only a few years earlier, in 1911, Price had joined forces with Father James Anthony Walsh of Boston to start a seminary that would become the training ground for the Catholic Foreign Mission Society of America—Maryknoll. Walsh was already the editor of *The Field Afar*, a missionary magazine aimed at American Catholics, which had first begun to publish in 1907, even before the mission society had started. This professionally edited publication became the principal means of publicity, financial support, and vocational appeal for Maryknoll.

After his encounter with Price and his companions, Keller became an avid reader of *The Field Afar*. In the following two years, Keller met twice with James Anthony Walsh, who paid annual visits to St. Patrick's. After the second visit, in 1920, Keller asked Walsh how to go about applying for Maryknoll. He was told that he had to obtain permission from Archbishop Edward Hanna of San Francisco, for whose diocese Keller had been studying. Hanna willingly gave the young man leave to enter Maryknoll, adding that he could return to his home diocese whenever he wished.

Keller's parents had become accustomed to the thought that he wanted to be a diocesan priest, but the idea of his going overseas alarmed them. However, since he was rapidly approaching his twenty-first birthday, parental permission was not an issue. Nevertheless, he managed to persuade them that this time he really knew his mind.

Full of exuberance, Keller boarded an east-bound train in August, 1921, for a two-week sightseeing trip that eventually brought him to the Maryknoll seminary at Ossining, thirty miles north of New York City. Maryknoll at that time was in a primitive state, consisting of four wooden farm buildings on a hill ("Mary's Knoll") several hundred feet above the Hudson River. The only modern building was a new fieldstone structure, which contained the offices of *The Field Afar*. A large fieldstone seminary was going up, but it would not be completed for years.

Twenty priests, perhaps a dozen brothers, and about sixty-five students made up the Maryknoll community in 1921. Life was rugged, but by all accounts filled with laughter. These young men (and nearly all were young) pitched into maintenance chores and helped take care of the pigs, cows, and chickens on the farm. Afternoons off meant hikes or bicycle rides in the surrounding Westchester hills. These early Maryknollers saw themselves as pioneers of a mighty movement that would spread their faith from America even as their country's global importance increased.

Keller was an average student, but his attention to spiritual duties and his ready laugh brought him admiration and popularity. He was an incessant note-taker on any and all subjects. He was also a bit naïve, and he became the butt of at least one professor's jibes, which Keller took good-naturedly.

The young man's enthusiasm for Maryknoll increased and remained high. To a professor at St. Patrick's, he wrote: "I think I would be justified in shooting anyone that would dare to take me away from here." To gain some medical experience for an eventual mission assignment, Keller spent the summer of 1922 at St. Vincent's Hospital in New York City. He worked as an orderly, went out on ambulance calls, and observed surgical techniques in the emergency room. Much of his free time was spent in the children's ward.

If Maryknoll could be called a family, James A. Walsh was unquestionably its father. Until the society had grown to the point where he could delegate some of his duties, he ran things almost single-handedly. He stayed as close to the seminarians as his other work permitted. He gave weekly conferences in which were discussed the progress and problems of missioners overseas, shared with them the knowledge of the society's shaky financial condition, and dispensed spiritual advice. He urged them to be bigger than their society.

Walsh's faithfulness to spiritual exercises—meditation, daily Mass, rosary, visits to the Blessed Sacrament—impressed Walsh's spiritual sons. It should be noted that the seminary schedule, based on the Particular Rule common to all Catholic houses of formation, was designed to assist in the training of young men who, as priests, would be rational, considerate, orderly, frugal, systematic, and obedient to Church authority. According to an unpublished doctoral thesis on the Maryknoll Fathers,[2] the Rule contained strong admonitions against "particular friendships." The study commented: "The result was that the seminarians formed no close friendships with anyone but attempted to be equally affable with a wide range of acquaintances." No Maryknoller fulfilled this ideal better than Keller, who was widely regarded in the society as the "perfect seminarian."

The feeling of being part of a family was common to all Maryknollers. When Keller became a publicist and fund-raiser for the society, he did it for men he knew and loved, whose ability to carry on their work overseas depended on his ability to find the wherewithal for them to do it. He looked forward to the day when he could join them in the "fields afar."

Shortly after being ordained subdeacon in June, 1923, Keller was assigned to study at the Catholic University in Washington, D.C., where he lived in a small house with several other Maryknollers. This was an assignment that allowed him to do research in the Library of Congress frequently, and take advantage of the city's cultural offerings. As a subdeacon, a cleric in major orders, he took upon himself the obligation of the daily recitation of the breviary and the promise of lifetime celibacy. He completed his theological studies at Catholic University and prepared for a master's degree in medieval history. With customary energy, Keller tried to complete his 15,000-word thesis on the rise and fall of the Latin Empire of Constantinople (1204–1261) in his first semester. He handed it in before Christmas. His professor, Dr. Peter Guilday, handed it back saying, "This will never do." A few months later, Keller turned in substantially the same paper. This time it was accepted, and Keller learned something about the workings of bureaucracy.

From Guilday, a distinguished historian of the American Church, he also learned that the meaning of historical trends was more important than individual facts. Keller also picked up from Guilday an enthusiasm for the convergence of cross and flag. "To understand the Catholic Church in America," Guilday wrote around this time, "one must see how naturally and integrally the spiritual allegiance of its members knit into the national allegiance so as to round each other out." Guilday was a proponent of the Americanist wing of the Church in the United States, which saw in this country's religious freedom the ideal climate for the spread of the faith. He was a follower of the nineteenth-century prelate, John Ireland of St. Paul, who sought to adapt Catholic practices to the American temperament as opposed to those bishops who tried to retain Old World languages and customs among the newly arrived immigrants. Ireland's philosophical thrust was particularly congenial to a man of Keller's point of view.

Archbishop Hanna visited Washington in 1924 and dropped in on his erstwhile seminarian. He suggested to Keller that he might wish to be ordained to the priesthood in his home diocese instead of at Maryknoll. This would save the Keller family much expense, ensure a larger turnout, and provide publicity for Maryknoll. Keller was surprised and delighted and picked his parish church, St. Francis de Sales, on August 15, 1925, for the ceremony. (It was unusual, then as now, for someone to be ordained in his home parish church.) Archbishop Hanna presided at the ordination, as he had promised. Keller sent this note to Walsh: ". . . a word of gratitude to you first of all to whom I owe so much. It was so pleasant to have the cheery greeting from Maryknoll. The archbishop was most gracious. I was hoping for a little earthquake to lend a bit of color to the day, but I still feel normal and most ready for my first Holy Sacrifice tomorrow morning."

At Keller's first Mass, there was again a large turnout of family and friends. The master of ceremonies was Charles McCarthy, another Maryknoller from the Bay area, two years younger than Keller. Also in attendance was Father Joseph McCormack, who headed the small Maryknoll house in San Francisco. As was the custom, only the family received Holy Communion from the new priest. Keller had received many monetary gifts on his ordination, and he used this money to pay off a bill for tuition, in the amount of $1,150, which his family still owed to the San Francisco seminary.

Now, instead of returning to Catholic University as he had expected, Keller received word from Walsh to stay where he was until further notice. Since he did not yet know what his mission assignment would be, he enjoyed a few weeks of relaxation and family visits. Then he heard that McCormack was being assigned to Manchuria and that he, as his nearest replacement, would take over the Maryknoll house in San Francisco.

He was young—only twenty-five—and untested. He had only a vague idea of what he was supposed to do, possessed no previous experience or handbook for guidance, but had ample room for the fullest exercise of his imagination and exuberance. This assignment to work in the United States, although he had no way of knowing it at the time, placed him in the field he would remain in permanently. Keller never received an overseas mission assignment from Maryknoll.

•3•

Endless Opportunities

"I am convinced that if we follow a policy of restrained publicity, we could do much to arouse mission interest that could be effected in no other way."

James Keller

The death of Thomas F. Price, Maryknoll's cofounder, in September, 1919, reduced the society's first band of missionaries in China to three. James Edward Walsh became their leader.[1] He, along with Ford and Meyer, rejoiced to see steady arrivals from the States in subsequent years swell their numbers to twenty-five priests and two brothers by 1927. Their mission, centered in the city of Kongmoon, encompassed a territory the size of Ohio with a population of six million. In the midst of civil war, bandit raids, flooding, dysentery, and superstition, their "mission impossible" was to convert the Chinese to Christianity and to reduce the human misery that nearly overwhelmed them. In 1927, a smallpox epidemic claimed the life of Father Daniel McShane, who had opened an orphanage to care for abandoned babies. That same year, James E. Walsh became the first American bishop in China.

Korea became Maryknoll's second foreign mission field in 1922. Like Kongmoon, it was a portion of an area staffed by the Paris Foreign Mission Society, which had suffered terrible losses in personnel during World War I. Encompassing the northern fifth of the country, the Penyang mission had a population of several million and was as large as Massachusetts, Connecticut, and Delaware combined. Its head, Father Patrick J. Byrne, led a contingent of seventeen priests and two brothers in 1927.

In 1925, the Paris Foreign Mission turned another large territory over to Maryknoll, this time in China. The Kaying mission, with a population of 2.5 million, came under the direction of Ford, one of the original four.

A portion of Manchuria, a huge area wrested from China by Japan in 1905, came under Maryknoll's care in 1926. Directed by Father Raymond A. Lane in the city of Fushun, the mission grew and prospered, although it was so cold in Manchuria that water cruets for Mass had to be heated to keep them from freezing. Maryknollers sometimes referred to their churches in areas such as Korea and Manchuria as "holy refrigerators."

Other Maryknoll commitments taken on during its first two decades of expansion (1918–1938) included a hostel for university students in Manila and a large parish in Honolulu. Maryknoll work started in Japan in a small way in 1933.

It cost the society about $400,000 a year to maintain its missionaries in the field, support the native seminaries and novitiates they started, and provide for the seminarians and priests at home. In addition, Maryknoll owed $800,000 for the construction of its headquarters building. To make the infant society better known to America's 20 million Catholics (1930 census figure), a small band of priests was assigned to stay behind to seek personnel and funding for Maryknoll's ambitious plans. This is where James Keller came in. He was not the only Maryknoller doing this job, but he was the most effective.

From 1925 to 1930, he criss-crossed the state of California and other parts of the West telling the story of his fellow Maryknollers' exploits and hardships. He spoke at six to ten parish Masses each Sunday, addressed Catholic societies, and delivered talks in high schools and colleges. He was a one-man cheering section for those who were propagating the faith overseas. In the jargon of missionary societies, his work was known as "propaganda" (from the Latin, meaning to propagate, or spread, the faith). Although the term has taken on sinister connotations in our time, there was nothing sinister about Keller's unremitting efforts to advance what he often referred to as the "noblest cause in the world." He was doing so well that the financially struggling society could not spare him for a mission post.

Keller spent the bulk of his time in and around San Francisco and Los Angeles, where he could see "almost endless opportunities among the wealthy class." In an average year, he logged more than 25,000 miles on the Southern Pacific Railroad, courtesy of a cost-free clergy pass. Keller had a passion for saving money that could be better used on the missions. With his old car on its last legs, he decided not to ask Maryknoll to buy him a new one. Instead, he encouraged six young socialites he had befriended to request donations from their friends. They raised enough for a Rolls-Royce, but Keller settled for a $650 Ford.

Keller's appearance and warm personality made him a hit with all classes of people, rich and poor, young and old. For example, since part of his job was to supervise the construction of Maryknoll's new residence for high school seminarians at Los Altos, thirty miles south of San Francisco, he found a way to kill two birds with one stone. By bringing college students to the residence to wash windows and do other chores, he both saved money and gave them a sense of participation in the society's work. Many of these young people remained lifetime supporters of Maryknoll. Keller himself talked to them only of his confreres who were doing the "real spiritual work" abroad. He invariably effaced himself.

Keller's cheerful persistence had its effect. Within three years, he recruited several dozen young men as vocation prospects. Receipts in San Francisco went up to $40,000 a year, and his initial probes into even wealthier Los Angeles yielded about half that amount. His most enduring contribution to the barely solvent society, however, was the Maryknoll Guild, later known as the sponsor system. He described its beginnings in his autobiography, *To Light a Candle:*

> As I gave my talks and tried to get support for Maryknoll's activities, I began to refer more and more often to this dollar-a-day need (for each missioner's support). I pointed out how helpful it would be if interested individuals would decide to support a missioner for one or more days each month. I made no specific requests and I carefully avoided obligating anyone to a particular sum or a special period of time. But to my great satisfaction, there were an increasing number of offers to help with monthly contributions that would defray per diem costs. . . . I emphasized that anyone signing up should feel free to discontinue his help at any time; also, that any help given to

Maryknoll should not interfere with personal or parish obligations.

The idea may have originated with Brother Luke de la Motte, who handled the accounts for the Maryknoll work in San Francisco. A convert to Catholicism, he had observed a similar practice in the Episcopal Church. Together he and Keller perfected the method, which included a reminder sent each month and an immediate acknowledgment to those who signed up to "sponsor a missioner." In order to clear all his decks, Keller informed Monsignor Cantwell, chancellor of the diocese, of his plan and obtained the chancellor's permission to go ahead. Subsequently, the society followed the same practice in every diocese where Maryknoll introduced the sponsor plan.

Although any willing Maryknoller could put the sponsor plan into effect with good results, the idea caught on slowly with other Maryknoll priests who were promoting the society. Many preferred to rely on church collections, which yielded a larger immediate gain. But Keller's innovation eventually prevailed. By 1934, about 2,500 sponsors averaging $2 per month, were providing $60,000 a year, a factor that kept the society from cutting back its missionary work during the Depression.

With no older priest nearby to talk to, Keller corresponded frequently with James Anthony Walsh back in Ossining. "I can only urge you," Walsh wrote, "to remember that you are not made of iron and that you are carrying an unusually heavy burden at the present time. As I have already advised you, remember that we can't take every opportunity that comes. Our work is full of opportunities and we are like people standing on the edge of mines, who realize that the more they dig, the more they gain. But no man can keep on digging day and night without exhausting his strength."

Keller shared his ambivalence about fund-raising with Walsh. As he carried his message of missionary heroism to the wealthy class in California, he must have felt a little like the prophet Jeremiah in Disneyland. To Walsh he described one socialite wedding to which he had been invited: "The whole gathering was made up of the most cultured and refined of the ultra-rich. But beautiful as all was, yet the emptiness of it all was so forcibly impressed on me.

It was an opportunity to see the very best that the world can give and to compare in contrast the privilege that is ours in keeping aloof from these things for another world. . . . Do not fear, however, that I have gotten the 'society bug'—or that I'll be spoiled—on the contrary, extremes seem to keep me in a fairly normal spiritual condition. . . . Yesterday afternoon I was in the midst of the most elaborate festivities I have ever seen. Last night I was hearing confessions for long hours and this morning I had to speak on propaganda at six Masses."

Keller's diffidence about asking directly for money, combined with his obvious enthusiasm, made it easy for people to contribute to Maryknoll. On one occasion, he was approached by a bank officer who told him, "I like your tactics. You do not ask, but you are getting so many friends just by that method. We are so tired of having the clergy dun us!" Keller gave the credit to Walsh for having impressed on him the practice of not "pushing" for money, but to do his best and rely on Providence.

Providence may have smiled on Keller as he strove to make Maryknoll a household word, but things did not go as smoothly on the home front. Being *de facto* superior on the West Coast, he had to mediate a long-simmering dispute between an officious Maryknoll sister and a grumpy brother who disagreed on the best way to handle the financial accounts at Los Altos. Keller humorously referred to himself as "a thorn between two roses." He backed the brother too strongly and was rebuked by Walsh for ignoring the sister's efficiency and other good qualities. Keller also had his hands full with an alcoholic missioner who had returned from China and would do no work for his room and board. It was months before he could get the priest returned to Ossining. Keller also had to contend with a diocesan priest in Los Angeles who thought Maryknoll was getting too much publicity. Thus, for a time, the society was barred from taking up any collections in the diocese. Keller came up with a face-saving compromise by which Maryknoll received whatever collections were due it and the priest got the credit he thought he deserved. Permission to speak in Los Angeles parishes was restored.

Keller enjoyed his work. To him it was "like winning a football game." But no one entered Maryknoll to remain in the United States. And Keller was no exception. In a typical letter to another

Maryknoller in 1928, he wrote: "Had hoped I would get the 'skids' this year and be sent to China on some real spiritual work—there is too much of the material about this."

But each year, new mission assignments would be made for overseas work. And each year, Keller would be disappointed to be kept in California.

So as a reward for a job well done, James Anthony Walsh gave his protégé, Keller, a first-hand look at the missions in 1928. Keller was assigned to accompany Bishop John J. Dunn, auxiliary bishop of New York, on a pilgrimage to Sydney, Australia, to take part in the worldwide Eucharistic Congress. Dunn was head of the National Society for the Propagation of the Faith office in New York, an organization charged with raising funds for the training and education of priests and catechists in mission lands.

"Your duties," wrote Walsh, "would be to look pleasant, give a few lectures *en route*, notify the Maryknollers ahead of time and turn a few somersaults."

Keller received free passage from the American Express Company for his part in securing passengers for the Matson liner *Ventura*. Leaving Father Charles F. McCarthy in charge of promotion work, Keller set sail on August 14, 1928. The next day, "sick as a canary," he was unable to celebrate Mass on the third anniversary of his ordination. He remained seasick during a good portion of the voyage.

Despite his queasy stomach, Keller lost no time in getting acquainted with everyone on the boat, which included a party of four bishops, twenty-three priests, and a good number of lay people on their way to Hawaii, Samoa, the Fiji Islands, and Sydney. Keller was placed at the bishops' table along with Dunn, Bishop Drumm of Des Moines, Bishop Heelan of Sioux City, and Bishop Schwertner of Wichita. "I found several advantages in dining with them," he wrote in his travel diary. One advantage was financial. Bishop Drumm handed the young priest a $1,000 check for Maryknoll. This generosity was matched by Father Cushman, pastor of Holy Trinity in New York, who settled himself in a deck chair next to the young Maryknoller. "He wanted to chat and I wanted to finish my letter," Keller wrote. "But I thought it better not to be selfish, so we chatted. Then came a checkbook out of his pocket. He wrote something on one of the leaves, tore it out of the book, handed it to me. Naturally I looked at the check out of the corner of my eye. It was for one thousand dollars. 'Use it for whatever you wish,' said Father Cushman. It pays to listen sometimes!" The Keller charm was obviously working with this wealthy pastor, who later gave Keller another $8,500 for Maryknoll.

After a short stay in Hawaii where local Maryknollers showed the sights to Bishop Dunn and some of the other clergy, the pilgrims—with a seasick James Keller—crossed the equator ("No signs on the ocean or anything") and put in at Pago Pago, "the wonder spot of the Samoan Islands." As the group toured the coconut groves, a wealthy woman from California promised Keller a $5,000 gift for Maryknoll on her return. In all, he raised nearly $20,000 on this trip—5 percent of the Society's annual budget. The Fiji Islands proved disappointing ("quite modern"), but the magnificent harbor at Sydney surpassed everyone's expectations.

The Eucharistic Congress opened on September 5 in the large, new Cathedral of St. Mary in the heart of the city. A crowd of 4,000 filled the edifice while 70,000 waited outside. It was a manifestation of strength in a country of six million, of whom about one-quarter were Catholic. Subsequent ceremonies turned out crowds of between 150,000 and 200,000. Sunday, September 9, was the final day of the congress. In his travel diary, Keller described it:

> At Manly Hall, the diocesan seminary on the opposite side of the harbor, a Solemn Pontifical Mass was celebrated by Archbishop Hanna of San Francisco. The Host was then consecrated. Shortly after lunch, the procession started, Cardinal Cerretti bearing the Monstrance. A beautiful yacht carried the Sacred Host with the Cardinal, Bishops and priests. The rest of the procession followed in other boats. As the yacht passed the entrance to the harbor, the Cardinal blessed the Seven Seas and all the world. Promptly on scheduled time the yacht docked on the mainland side of the harbor, and the great procession began the triumphant march. What a sight it was! As far as one could see, the streets were massed with people. Nearly a million lined the way of march. Not one thing marred the solemnity. It was the greatest manifestation that Sydney had ever seen.

The worldwide scope of the Catholic Church was not lost on this young priest. "My trip is teaching me so much already," he wrote from Sydney late in September. "More than anything else, it has made me realize what a tiny cog one is in the great work of the Church. And, now, at a distance from my bit of work, I can see many ways in which I can improve and profit by past mistakes."

The three weeks in Australia were not all pomp, ceremony, and visiting with Church dignitaries. Keller spent some time with the family of Mark Foy, owner of one of the largest department stores in Sydney. Two of his daughters had gone to school in California, where they had met Keller. The Foys treated him royally, showing him around the countryside where they had houses scattered. They visited the prehistoric Jenolon Caves and spent a weekend at a hotel in the Blue Mountains. The Foys gave their "American cousin" a generous donation for the missions and, for himself, a packet of Mother Sills' pills for his *mal de mer*. Even Mother Sills couldn't keep the gremlins quiet in his stomach.

It took twenty days to sail from Sydney to Singapore, with stops at Batavia (now Djakarta, capital of Indonesia) and other ports. Keller stayed close to Bishop Dunn, who liked the American mission unit so much that he had been dubbed the "Maryknoll Bishop." The two steered clear of most of the tourist traps and plunged into the native quarters to get some taste of mission life.

One night in Batavia, Dunn and Keller set out, with the aid of a local guide, to see the native quarter. It proved to be almost more than they had bargained for. The three stepped gingerly through a dark alley that took them into a dingy marketplace filled with the forms of men sleeping in strange, contorted positions. Curiosity soon gave way to fear. Keller reported:

> Next we were piloted up a dark lane past tiny shacks that were patched together in tenement fashion. We saw a torch in a dingy shop. We peered in and, in the dim light, we were greeted by the smiling faces of two Chinese. They should have been tucked away in bed instead of prowling about at that hour—but I guess they thought the same of us too! Onward we plodded in the darkness. I was thinking of the dangers we were exposing ourselves to. What if some stray native should tap us over the head in the hope of finding a few stray dollars in our thin wallets, or if—then came a crash and a yell—what was it? I turned and there was the Bishop of New York sprawling down in a deep ditch on the side of the narrow path. No, he hadn't been hit.

He had tripped. We helped him back and then decided that we
had had enough of nocturnal touring.

In his diary, Keller deplored the plight of "almost 50 million
souls" in the Dutch East Indies, "practically all of them in the
darkness of paganism or Mohammedanism." He found little ro-
mance or poetry in the condition of the people—"men working like
beasts in the blazing sun of the tropics." Keller was touched in
particular by the lot of women, and contrasted it with the place
given to woman by Jesus Christ.

The priest concluded his reflections on what he had just witnessed:

> Why have they been cheated out of the blessings that Christ
> sent to them 20 centuries ago? Men in thousands have come to
> their lands to gain for themselves. But how few have gone to
> help these peoples—to bring them to the blessings that others
> in the past have brought to us! Would that others could have
> the glimpse into their lives that it has been our privilege to have.
> Surely then, more would take an interest in them.

At Singapore, the pair caught a German boat bound for Hong
Kong, where the first Maryknollers had debarked just ten years
before. They were greeted by James E. Walsh, now a bishop, at
the Maryknoll Center House. Ford and Meyer, the remaining members of the original group of four, were upcountry—too far for a
visit. Dunn and Keller did get a glimpse of life in South China by
looking in on missions in the Hong Kong region, notably a leprosarium at Shek Lung. All the while, Keller was making home
movies on his camera. He combined these with some commercial
footage he had bought on his journey and had the two sets of movies
edited into a film he was to use in conjunction with his mission
talks back in the States. Perhaps in this way, he felt, the people at
home would get some idea of the missionary work to be done in
the Orient. In the film, he took particular note of the damage
inflicted by the Chinese Communists wherever they went. Keller's
anti-Communism, like that of many other Maryknollers, was no
post–World War II phenomenon. It was rooted in the experiences
of missionaries for at least two decades before the outbreak of the
war.

Dunn and Keller continued by boat to Shanghai, Tientsin, inland to Peking, and then across the Yellow Sea to Manchuria, where they saw Father Lane and other Maryknollers. On their voyage home, they made stops in Korea and Japan.

The four-month journey had a lasting effect on the twenty-eight-year-old priest. It brought to his speaking engagements the vividness of first-hand impressions; it reinforced his dedication to the missions, in which he now saw Maryknoll as a small part of a worldwide apostolate; it filled him with grudging admiration for the dedication of Communist party members, especially in China. The timing of this extensive trip—the longest of his life—could not have been better. It took place just before the horizons of his own work were to extend beyond the boundaries of California and take in an entire nation.

• 4 •

The Search for a System

"Almost eight years ago, I started experimenting and quickly came to the conclusion that all that was necessary for success, outside the grace of God, was to systematize efforts and follow out details."

James Keller

More than pleased with Keller's performance on the high seas in 1928, his superior, Walsh, wrote:

> Propaganda on trip seems to be quite effective. Father Mc-Carthy has been working hard on the card party, which has exceeded his expectations and apparently reached $2,000. But from Fr. Cushman alone you have gotten half that amount in one evening! Perhaps we ought to keep you at sea, changing from one group of tourists to another!

Charles McCarthy, one of Keller's chief assistants during these California years (1925–1930), shared the latter's tireless quest for high achievement, but without Keller's stamina or personality. Despite admonitions from Keller and Walsh, McCarthy drove himself too hard, with the result that he had to be hospitalized for one ailment after another. McCarthy's health problems opened a rift between the two men that never healed.

Early in 1930, Keller sent this frank assessment to Walsh:

> Father McCarthy—trouble in getting him to take things easy. . . . If he doesn't follow [instructions], we'll have a per-

25

manent invalid on our hands. . . . Fr. Charlie is a splended priest, has many valuable qualities, and I am counting on him as a most desirable assistant if I am to continue my present work. He could relieve me of so many little details that consume so much of my time. . . . The good little fellow is miles ahead of me in many ways, but in the way of personal contacts and results God may have blessed me with a little advantage. Charlie has tried his best to do the same as I have in this regard, and his inability has disappointed him a little more than he is conscious of. I have given him several opportunities and leads, but he doesn't "make the grade." He not only realizes this, but he sees so many things come easy to me . . . and I fear it has made him a bit jealous. He has tried to imitate me too much, whereas if he developed his own sweet qualities, he might be much more valuable to the Society than me.

The condescension with which Keller regarded him, clearly evident in this letter, must have grated on McCarthy's sensitive nature. Although he eventually recovered from his kidney ailments and other illnesses to become one of the architects of Maryknoll's public relations and vocation efforts for the next quarter century, the relationship between himself and Keller was never comfortable. The two men worked together efficiently over the years, but there is little evidence of warmth between them.

A Maryknoller for whom Keller did feel both admiration and affection was John J. Considine. From 1924 to 1935, Considine was stationed in Rome, where he established the Fides News Service to disseminate mission information. Two years older than Keller, Considine was the one person, outside of Walsh himself, to whom Keller could unburden himself and be assured of a sympathetic hearing for his grand plans. On the level of missionary scholarship, Considine had no peer in Maryknoll, and few Americans could match his grasp of global strategy. Over the years, he held a number of positions of authority in Maryknoll, traveled widely, and wrote a number of highly respected books. The Maryknoll triumvirate of Considine, McCarthy, and Keller was responsible for the wide acceptance of mission thinking among American Catholics that emanated from Maryknoll.

Besides McCarthy, Keller had other Maryknoll priest-assistants during his California assignment. Of Father John Martin, he said:

"a good priest, willing and generous." For many years, Martin headed the Maryknoll house in St. Louis, where he was responsible for many vocations. Another assistant was Father William Cummings, in whom Keller saw "fine possibilities," that were handicapped by "abrupt mannerisms and an air of self-sufficiency." Cummings later went to the Philippines where he died on a Japanese prison ship during World War II. Father William Kress was "of no specific help" to Maryknoll's promotion work. He went on to the Maryknoll Japanese mission in Los Angeles and then to Hawaii. Father Richard Rhodes didn't last very long either. He rubbed Keller the wrong way by arriving at his post with a demand for a two-month vacation before beginning work. Keller had good things to say about Father William Coulehan, who was to succeed him on the West Coast, and Father Hugh Lavery, who spent much of his life with the Japanese mission.

Father Norman Batt was a special case. A combative sort, he caught onto the work of promotion quite well, but never liked it. Coulehan recounts that "Father Batt arrived this morning. He is so disgusted with propaganda that he is thinking of starting a Society that does not have that kind of work—and where they have no Kellers!" Despite their differences, Batt and Keller remained friendly "sparring partners." Batt became a teacher of biology in Maryknoll formation houses (seminaries) and supervised much of the society's construction work.

Personality problems plagued the California headquarters during this phase of Maryknoll's growth, some of them caused by Keller's seeming inability to slow down long enough to train his assistants thoroughly. But the main problem was that of organization. Decisions in California had to be cleared with Maryknoll headquarters in New York. Keller's own authority was vague, a fact about which he often complained. In response to one such protest about vagueness of his position, Keller received this reply from Walsh: "Official status—the past success of your present somewhat anomalous position is sufficient warrant for its continuance."

The situation was clarified, on paper at least, after the Maryknoll Chapter (a sort of constitutional assembly) met in August 1929. The body, drawn from delegates in mission areas, confirmed Walsh as Superior General, and elected Patrick Byrne, James Drought, William O'Shea, and Raymond Lane as members of his General

Council. Keller received this communication from Walsh: "In our recent Council meeting, you were assigned as director of propaganda for the Mid-West and Pacific Coast—this while retaining your present position as superior at Los Altos."

As superior, Keller acted as "point man," arousing interest and enthusiasm in Maryknoll. He spent as much time as he could showing his China movie in schools. His assistants, one or more, would then follow up his efforts by counseling any students who showed an inclination to become a foreign missionary. A system was being created and, by 1930, the Los Altos formation house held seventy-five budding foreign missioners. Meanwhile, Maryknoll had just been invited to open a house for aspirants in Cincinnati by Archbishop John T. McNicholas,[1] as could be inferred from Walsh's letter to Keller.

During his first visit to Cincinnati, in 1929, Keller had no sooner seen the archbishop than he was laid up with an attack of appendicitis. McNicholas came to his bedside and the whole affair provided the busy promoter with a much-needed rest. The extent to which he (Keller) had been driving himself can be appreciated from his mother's importunate letter to Walsh:

> I thought it advisable to drop you a few lines about my dear son, Father James. Since his recent operation, he has telegraphed and written, and in both messages he has said that he would be back at work soon again. I know that he will do just what he says, and I feel that you are the only one that can stop him until he has a complete rest, and is ready to start out with his zealous work again. It may be a little presumptuous on my part in suggesting this to you, but he is far away from home, and among strangers, and this is why I am asking you to advise him.

A year later, Keller was again in Cincinnati when word reached him that his father had just died of a heart attack. Keller, Sr., after attending Sunday Mass with the Knights of Columbus, had been stricken at home where he called his wife and four children to his side, asking them not to leave the room. They were with him when he died. Only three weeks before, he had accompanied his priest son to a parish church in Oakland to assist him in a preaching engagement.

The funeral for Keller's father was attended by hundreds, including fifty priests. But James was not there. It would have taken him four days to reach home by train. The family agreed that he should remain in Cincinnati and complete his work. Keller's sense of loss was softened by the arrival in Cincinnati of James A. Walsh. "I cannot tell you," he wrote later, "what a consolation it was to be with you for the two days after I heard of the death of my dear father. It was a blessing from God and took away the sharpness of the natural sorrow—to have my only other earthly father so near."

Back in Oakland a few months later, Keller accompanied his mother to his father's grave. In a heartfelt tribute to his father, Keller wrote to Walsh: "Poor Dad led a very simple life in the background, but he was always so constantly cheerful and good-natured—and never unkind. He will always be an ideal to me."

Keller almost lost his other "earthly father" in the summer of 1930 when Walsh was seriously injured in an auto crash. Besides his concern over Walsh's injuries, Keller had the added worry over possibly losing the opportunity to obtain a house for Maryknoll in Los Angeles that would provide a base for effective promotion work. With Walsh on the sidelines, Keller's dealings with Maryknoll had to be conducted with Father Patrick Byrne, Walsh's second-in-command. Byrne was not inclined to grant Keller much freedom of action.

At the time of Walsh's accident, Keller was combing the city in search of an accessible headquarters. He chafed at the remote location of the promotion center, which was part of Maryknoll's Japanese Mission on the south side of the city. This center, on South Boyle Street, served the needs of the Japanese very well, but potential contributors would rarely venture there.

After an intensive investigation, Keller located a twelve-room house on a main street (South Alvarado) near a streetcar line. He found that he could buy it for $19,000, but he was unable to persuade Byrne that it was worth the investment. Acting on his own, Keller borrowed $400 from a friend, added $100 of his own, and secured a thirty-day option on the property.

As the time approached for the expiration of the option, Keller bombarded the Maryknoll General Council with letters urging them to reconsider their negative decision. Byrne, who was running the society at the time, partially relented. He said the society would be willing to rent the Alvarado Street house for one year, but that did not satisfy the owner, who wanted a quick sale. Keller offered to find a third party, who would purchase the property on the understanding that Maryknoll would take it over in a year or two. He received encouragement from Walsh, who had recovered sufficiently to lend Keller some support—but there was no absolute assurance.

Heartened by this slight change of attitude, Keller cleared two potential obstacles to any final arrangement. He obtained permission from the bishop of Los Angeles, John Cantwell, and from the local pastor, to operate in their territory. "It has been almost like a football game," he wrote, "and we are getting very near the end of the last quarter. Many a game has been won in less time. We won't go down without fighting!"

On the day before the thirty-day option expired, Keller pulled his rabbit out of a hat. He arranged for a local bank to assume a $12,000 mortgage on the property—and he found a benefactor to lend Maryknoll $7,000 in cash at 6 percent interest. The society was obliged, in turn, to pay a modest rental for a year or two, after which it would exercise its option to buy. Keller was supremely confident that the sharp increase in Maryknoll income deriving from the use of the house would persuade the Maryknoll Council to make the purchase two years hence. As it turned out, he was right.

As if to celebrate that "famous victory," several months later, Keller accepted an invitation to the Notre Dame–University of Southern California football game in the Rose Bowl and saw the Fighting Irish pull off a last-minute triumph. "The USC–ND game taught me lessons aplenty!" he wrote to Walsh. "There is always much hope even on the gloomiest days. And it is always so much fun when things turn out just like the ND score did, and thanks to the dear Lord, I know of scarcely one instance where the results have not been almost the equivalent!"

The ink was scarcely dry on the legal papers for the new house when Keller began to make things happen. He found a paying boarder—his brother Reg, who had come south as a Cadillac salesman. He arranged with the phone company for an easy-to-remember number (EXposition 2100) and had the house number changed to an equally easy 1220 S. Alvarado. If people couldn't reach him, it wouldn't be because he hadn't paved the way for them.

Instead of buying the necessities for the house, Keller let his supporters know what was needed. In poured donations of bed linen, altar vestments, candlesticks, dishes, and—from the Biltmore Hotel—furniture. He noted with a touch of pride that he had received more visitors in one day in the new location than had come to the previous address in six months. By making personal calls on the editors, Keller managed to place stories about the new mission house in three Los Angeles newspapers.

Keller even hired a former newspaper reporter to plant stories about Maryknoll in the local press. This worked very well until Walsh got wind of it and told him to abandon this little sideline. In many ways, Walsh was a priest of the old school.

Becoming known in Los Angeles was no easy matter, but Keller managed it by persuading several wealthy women to hold receptions for the benefit of Maryknoll in their large and luxurious houses. In this way, he could acquaint as many as 500 curiosity-seekers with tales of missionary hardship and heroism in South China. Events like these translated into the dollars that would keep Father Joe Sweeney from having to turn away lepers from his leprosarium in Kongmoon.

Walsh, often concerned about Keller's drive to do everything himself, urged him to "try and organize your work so it will not depend so much on your personality. When the time comes to replace you, a different individual with a different personality will naturally find it difficult unless the work is organized to stand on its merits." In response, and in an effort to let his fellow promoters know what he found to be the secret of his accomplishment, Keller set down these thoughts:

> I am conscious of different kinds of pride within me that I have not yet overcome. One variety is that of being sensitive to "asking for money." I never seem to disregard it as I should. So I have gotten into the habit of "beating around the bush" when I wanted to get something. . . . In other words, build up the fire, but always leave it to the other person to put the match to it. Of great importance also is to sincerely seek the friendship of the benefactor rather than what he or she has. This is often a weary task, especially when this interest must be genuine. Pretended friendship or interest is immediately detected as hypocritical, and it does not get far. It means that one has to keep

alive to opportunities, to be thoughtful (—visits of a few moments, a disinterested phone call, a little greeting or postcard, etc.) are responsible for many thousands of dollars that we have received in S.F. We are certainly not ordained to be diplomats, but still if we refuse to be, or at least try to be diplomatic, we simply cut ourselves off from the help that could be ours at the cost of such little effort.

To illustrate alertness to opportunities, Keller gave the example of a telegram he had sent to a wealthy woman on her birthday. Although they hardly knew each other, "she must have gotten a real kick out of it, for she came all the way from her home in Beverly Hills . . . to tell me how much she appreciated the remembrance." The woman left $200, which would provide food and shelter for a lot of Chinese refugees.

On another occasion, Keller had to be something of an acrobat. At a social function, he spotted Sir George MacDonald, a generous benefactor to Catholic causes. Going a safe distance from the unsuspecting philanthropist, Keller hopped over a hedge and "casually" bumped into him. His gymnastics were repaid with an appointment to visit Sir George.

A curious mixture of enjoyment and uneasiness colored Keller's approach to his work. Although he relished the challenge of his assignment, he confessed that he would "rather face any Chinese bandit" than ask for money. More than once, he reminded Walsh: "I shall always be happy to go anywhere or to do anything at anytime that you and your Council wish. Sometimes I long for work with souls that would be found on the missions. . . ."

Reacting to criticism from other Maryknollers that he stressed the material side of the work too much, Keller admitted to Walsh: "Probably I do, and it worries me a bit. . . . However, I have tried always to keep my motives higher than material ones. . . . My chief ambition has been to win good-will and friendships for the Society. From these contacts I thought vocations and financial help would come in a more generous manner."

Keller was too much of a visionary to confine his thinking to a state the size of California (even with Cincinnati thrown in). In 1930, he wrote a long letter to Walsh outlining a plan for the advance of vocational recruitment and financial support on a nationwide scale. In broad outline, it became the basis for Maryknoll's spread throughout the country, though it took another twenty years to accomplish. He cited the rise of junior colleges in California and proposed that Maryknoll imitate this educational trend. He had in mind the acquisition of large private homes in eight major cities (Cincinnati, Philadelphia, Boston, Detroit, Chicago, Cleveland, New York, and St. Louis) where twenty-five to thirty high school students would live while attending local Catholic institutions. Each house would be staffed by two priests, one exclusively for the students and the other to do promotion work. He cited the advantages:

—a Maryknoll Center in each or most of the large cities;
—an abundance of vocations which would not otherwise be had;
—better opportunity to select vocations and to easily eliminate undesirables;
—distribution of expense for building; equipment and maintenance to sections where assistance can be easily had if we made the effort "to go and get it";
—minimum of expense in outlay for building and equipment.

He added other advantages, most of which were aimed at making Maryknoll a "local cause" rather than something far away.

Father Walsh scribbled across Keller's letter: "Very fine idea on prep schools and propaganda support."

With the work in Los Angeles off to a good start, Keller began dreaming again—this time about New York. He broached the subject with Walsh in his letter of November 15, 1931:

Is there even a remote possibility of opening a propaganda center there? For years I have thought of the countless opportunities that it presents—that it is so close to the Center—that it could be made to care for possibly all the expense of the Center in time, not to speak of the immense opportunities that would be bound to follow from wills as the result of proper contacts. The thought of it has come to me repeatedly and I am praying that God may see fit to let us realize this opportunity. . . . I suppose I would not be able for it, but if you could not spare anyone who would be better fitted, I would be willing to take the responsibility.

He returned to the subject two days later, adding further reasons for his transfer to New York:

> Apart from the endless opportunities in NYC, it occurred to me also that it would be very helpful for me to be working directly under the Center. Our "system" could then be observed at close hand to see if it warrants encouragement—and if it does, its weaker points could be bolstered up by advice from those with more experience.

Keller was told to stay put in his western outpost for at least another year, but Walsh's reply gave him encouragement. Undaunted, he soon returned to the subject with the suggestion that he take some time the following summer to scout New York for a suitable location. Some six years before (in 1925) Maryknoll had sold a small residence on East 57th Street to finance the purchase of a house in Rome. (Religious societies habitually maintain some staff in Rome for the conduct of business with the Vatican.) It was there, on the Via Sardegna, that Considine and one or two others lived.

As it turned out, Keller didn't have to make a scouting trip to New York. Julia Ward, an internationally known fashion designer and a friend of Walsh, offered Maryknoll the use of a two-room apartment at 16 East 48th Street, two blocks from St. Patrick's Cathedral.

Meanwhile, Keller kept up his pace in California, recruiting sponsors and future missioners, and even conducting a tour for Mr. and Mrs. Yamamoto, an influential Japanese couple. And he almost officiated at the marriage of his sister Hazel to Thomas McCabe. He explained to Walsh the reason he couldn't make it:

> My broken rib—you'll laugh when I tell you how I got it—it was at the Jonathan Beach Club on a surf board, if you please! Nice way for a missioner to be cutting up! But it was on a contact job with some very wealthy people—they paid all the hospital bills, etc.—and from all the results that have come from the mishap, I guess it was a *"felix culpa"* ["happy fault"] that it happened.

The *"felix culpa"* prevented Keller from traveling north for the wedding, much to the disappointment of Hazel and her groom.

By August 1931, Keller felt that he had established a system that would enable other Maryknollers to carry on the work he had started. He wrote Walsh:

> During the past year, we made considerable progress in putting the work of general propaganda here on the Coast in such a condition that it does not depend for its success on any one person and so would not suffer greatly if any one person was withdrawn. Within this coming year, the work should be well enough established to "check me out" and plant me on the other side of the Pacific or any other place you wish.

Meanwhile, back East, Charles McCarthy had one final relapse so serious that he was anointed. Keller noted that in the year since the two had seen each other, McCarthy had written him but once— and that the letter was tinged with icy formality.

When the expected appointment to begin work in New York arrived, Keller's bags were half-packed. He spent the month of November consulting with Walsh and others at the Maryknoll headquarters near New York, and in preparing the way for his new assignment. He strongly proposed less reliance on the general mail appeals for funds and more attention to his own method of "personal contact."

Keller requested two or three priests to work with him in the Northeast, where one-quarter of the country's population was to be found. "If three of us have been kept quite busy in California," he noted, "it seems reasonable that at least as many are needed for an area with ten times more Catholics."

He sounded a note familiar to anyone whoever knew him: "Prospects will seldom come to us—we must 'go out after them'—and try by various means to force upon them an impression of our Cause that will not be lost in the 101 other interests that besiege them."

Then Keller headed west to wind up affairs in California and to celebrate Christmas with his family—his last. The concrete canyons of New York glittered in his eyes. They were to become his home for the rest of his days.

•5•

New York, New York

*"Within a radius of about five hours from New York City
there is probably one-third or one-quarter of the population
of the whole country."*

James Keller

James Anthony Walsh dropped a pebble into the pond, and left
it to Keller to make waves of his own. The pebble was Walsh's
introduction of Keller to Louise Hoguet, which took place in November 1931. Mrs. Hoguet, the wife of Robert Hoguet, a well-
known lawyer and banker, and the mother of eight children, made
her mark by conducting one of the grandest salons in New York,
a place where people came to meet intellectual French abbés, pen-
niless poets, famous philosophers, and other interesting personages.
At a time when rich Catholics were out to make a dollar and poor
ones were struggling to survive, Mrs. Hoguet valued the life of the
mind. Walsh's introduction was all Keller needed. She took an
immediate liking to the boyish priest from California.

Once he was settled in the building owned by Julia Ward on
48th Street, Keller lost no time in getting in touch with his new
acquaintance. One January day in 1932, he phoned Mrs. Hoguet.
Within an hour she was on the rickety elevator that led to Keller's
cubbyhole office/apartment on the fifth floor. She was forthright.
"What do you want me to do to help you?" she asked. Keller told
her he wanted to deliver the message of Maryknoll to New York's
most influential people. The following Sunday, he was a luncheon
guest at the Hoguets' large home on East 92nd Street where he met
a dozen generous givers to Catholic causes. Among them was Mrs.

36

Nicholas Brady, at whose Long Island home Cardinal Pacelli, the future Pope Pius XII, would be entertained during his American tour.

It was a good start, but only the beginning. Louise Hoguet drew up a list of about 300 people who, in her opinion, would show special interest in Maryknoll's religious and humanitarian work in the troubled Orient. During that winter of 1932, for example, Japanese troops were gradually taking over Manchuria where about two dozen Maryknollers had established the mission of Fushun. Keller worried about the safety of his missioner brothers caught in the unrest, even as he tried to watch his table manners and turn the dinner conversations to the subject of missionary work. It wasn't always easy. About a year later, Keller wrote to Walsh:

> Many of these people have to live in such a worldly atmosphere . . . that we feel it is a real help to them to take an interest in Maryknoll. They give their time and attention and money to so many empty things from which they get little or no return that we feel it is doing them a real favor to help them along to interest in God and souls.

But to Considine in Rome, Keller would admit his occasional discouragement. "Every now and again," he wrote, "I get rather fed up on this begging business, but with the help of the Lord, I seem to keep plodding along and, thanks to Him entirely, meeting with a success that even surprises me."

Keller's attitude toward his work could be summed up in an entry he made in his work diary in 1934: "I frequently keep before me the words of St. Gregory Nazianzen: 'Let him that hath access to the rich fear damnation if he get not the rich to help the poor.' "

In the early 1930s, Keller spent most of his days in the city visiting pastors, writing letters, and using the telephone; nights were set aside for dinners given by Mrs. Hoguet or other patrons. If he ate alone, it was usually in a distinctly unfashionable Child's restaurant or the 42nd Street Horn & Hardart Automat, where a meal cost about 55 cents. Moving among the wealthy did not cause Keller to abandon a simple lifestyle. He often went to Maryknoll headquarters in Ossining, to consult with Walsh and experiment with new techniques for mail campaigns. He also suggested story ideas for *The Field Afar*.

But it was Keller's weekends that were most exhausting. He traveled about the Northeast talking about Maryknoll at six to ten parish Masses every Sunday. Until Keller came on the scene, the Archdiocese of Boston was closed to Maryknoll. The imperious cardinal of Boston, William O'Connell, did not like religious societies, and he would not be swayed even by the persuasive James Anthony Walsh, a native son. When Keller gave it a try, he couldn't help but be intimidated by O'Connell and the huge dog that accompanied him everywhere he went. (It is said that the mastiff even ate his dinner from the priests' table at the cardinal's residence.) Twice in one evening Keller asked O'Connell for permission to let Maryknollers speak in the parishes of Boston, and twice he was turned down. Then, as he wrote to Considine: "I decided to try a third time, and much to my surprise, he said: 'You may have my permission.' " Was it Keller's undeniable charm or his gentle persistence that won the day? Perhaps both.

Maryknollers who followed Keller in promotion work spoke in awe about the day he wrested this permission from the formidable O'Connell, an accomplishment that even their revered founder had been unable to swing.

Once O'Connell's stamp of approval had been secured, Keller put the New York social scene behind him for a while and knocked on rectory doors in Boston to line up church dates. Pastors could still say no, and many of them, faced with hard economic times, turned Keller down. Others, however, were receptive, perhaps because they knew Walsh and a large number of other Maryknollers who had lived in Boston.

For his Sunday appearances in Boston, Keller would get into his Ford on Saturday mornings for the 200-mile drive each week to a different church. On Sunday afternoons, his work completed, he would drive back to Maryknoll in Ossining where he would leave the receipts and *Field Afar* subscriptions to be processed. He made the most of his time on the road planning the coming week's activities, listening to the Metropolitan Opera broadcast, or saying the rosary. A Maryknoll seminarian who knew him at Los Altos said that he used the notches on the steering wheel of his car to count the Our Fathers and Hail Marys. On Monday mornings, he drove down to the city and was at his desk at 9 A.M.

As he had done in California, Keller established a workable system of promotion in the East, one that did not depend on him alone. Coulehan and Cummings, his successors on the West Coast, were doing effective work, but it took time to get things organized in New York. By the end of 1933, Keller had raised $50,000 for the missions, with help on Sundays from his friendly critic, Norman Batt. With little effect, Keller asked Maryknoll for four or five priests to do the job properly.

In a typical letter to Walsh, Keller wrote: "We cannot blame anyone but ourselves if we do not take advantage of the opportunities. Our only need is for a few men assigned to this part of the work: average type is all that is needed, with a fair amount of zeal and willingness to take pains."

Wherever he went, Keller pushed the sponsor idea. His diary is filled with the names of people—well-known and unknown—who signed up to support a Maryknoller for thirty days a month, at one dollar a day. Before he had any salaried staff to help him in New York, he persuaded high school and college students to volunteer to send out personal reminders to the growing number of monthly contributors. To improve his managerial skills, he studied office procedure manuals from Chrysler and General Motors; to enhance his speaking ability, he took elocution lessons from a Doctor Sullivan, whose "Voice of Culture" sessions were popular. Keller never became a polished speaker, but earnestness and enthusiasm made up for any technical shortcomings.

A reliable source of volunteer help was found in the schools conducted by the Religious of the Sacred Heart of Jesus, an order of sisters who educated the daughters of wealthy Catholic families. Later, in his travels across the country, Keller often used the educational institutions of the Madames of the Sacred Heart, as they were called, as his base of operations. One woman who heard him talk to her college class remembered that Keller had a "happy voice." Another recalled that tears came to his eyes and he had to turn away from his audience to recover his composure when he spoke of a Maryknoller who had been kidnapped and killed by bandits in China. His sincerity was obvious.

Keller's closeness to the center of Maryknoll's operations enabled him to profit from the personal advice and direction of Walsh and, to a lesser extent, that of other members of the General Council, a sort of governing board. He admitted that his six years in California had had a narrowing effect on him, and he became less demanding of the priests who assisted him. "I confess I had expected too much," he told Walsh. He also reassured Walsh that he was keeping up his regular prayer habits and taking care of his health. He was learning to pace himself, as this entry from his diary indicates:

> Lots of invitations to luncheons and dinners . . . but we make it a practice to turn thumbs down on them if nothing more than food is in the proposition. It's much more fun sitting at home over a cheese sandwich than listening to some "pain in the neck" chatter of people who will spread themselves for a meal, but that's all.

At the same time, Keller attended a good number of weddings and dinners. He justified his attendance at these as "they usually make it possible to do more contact work in a couple of hours than would be possible in a couple of weeks." Nevertheless, he generally avoided late-night gatherings, which he found "too worldly for my thin blood." Keller's blood pressure was on the low side and he tried to make up for it, not always successfully, by getting extra sleep.

An admirer of some aspects of the free enterprise system, Keller tried to study its methods of sales and marketing so as to adapt them to his spiritual mission. He proposed to Maryknoll's General Council that the society take out a full-page ad in *Fortune* magazine, the bible of business executives. Despite the fact that Erwin Wasey, the public relations firm that handled the General Motors account, offered to prepare the ad without charge, Keller's request was turned down by the Council. He couldn't even persuade his superiors to run regular ads in the Catholic press offering information on wills. It was not that Keller was blind to the flaws of capitalism (the unemployment all around him made them self-evident), but he did pay tribute to the businessman's desire to promote his product aggressively. Keller was also strongly aware of the shortcomings of

Communism, but here too he admired the zeal of Karl Marx's followers. He was above all a pragmatist, though a principled one.

Keller, of course, realized that "pushing his product" involved vocations as well as collecting money and subscriptions. In schools and colleges, he hoped his appeal for missioners would fall on fertile ground. But gradually he broadened his appreciation of the meaning of the word "vocation." One day in 1933, Keller spoke to the students of the Sacred Heart Academy in Noroton, Connecticut, urging them to leave the world better than they had found it. For the first time he used the term "Christophers" to describe those who worked for the spiritual and material betterment of the world. (The term "Christopher" comes from the Greek and means "Christ-bearer.") In arriving at this concept, he was undoubtedly influenced by the example of capitalists aggressively selling their products and Communists promoting their ideas. Keller was caught by a vision of the followers of Christ—not just those in the religious life or on the missions—as active apostles in the advancement of the Gospel. It was a vision that never left him.

Keller's vision was a general one. During the 1930s, he never got down to particulars. Others, like Father Charles Coughlin of Royal Oak, Michigan, became deeply involved in politics, first supporting President Roosevelt and later condemning him. Rejecting partisan politics and concentrating on sharing the lives of the poor while feeding the hungry were the Catholic Worker communities, inspired by Peter Maurin and Dorothy Day. Somewhere in between Coughlin on the right and the Catholic Worker groups on the left was Msgr. John A. Ryan, head of the Social Action Department of the National Catholic Welfare Conference. Ryan was basically in agreement with the New Deal and served on various government commissions. The thirties was a period when many Catholics of various political colorations believed that, armed with their doctrine and the papal encyclicals, they had the answers to the problems of the modern world—though they disagreed strongly on what those answers were to be. Keller shared the widespread concern about the plight of the world, but circumstances prevented him from doing much about social problems, aside from exhorting his audience to become involved in contemporary affairs.

By temperament and out of experience, Keller believed in stressing the positive, a factor that kept him somewhat removed from the controversies of the day. His attitude reflected the Chinese motto he had picked up from some unknown source: "It is better to light one candle than to curse the darkness." That bit of Oriental wisdom had first lodged in his mind in 1933 when he accompanied an official of the Metropolitan Opera Company into the darkened opera house to discuss arrangements for a musical performance that would benefit Maryknoll. The official, Earle Lewis, led Keller into the darkened theater and asked him to wait in the orchestra while he went ahead to turn on the stage lights. In order to avoid hitting a piece of scenery, Lewis struck a match, Keller was impressed at the power of one little match to push back the darkness enough for Lewis to find the main switch that illuminated the vast space.

"The sight of that tiny flame," Keller recounted in his autobiography, "made an indelible impression on me. Insignificant as it was, it was greater than all the darkness. All that was needed to banish the darkness completely was to multiply that flicker of light. . . . In a human way it echoed the divine advice of St. Paul . . . 'Be not overcome by evil, but overcome evil with good.' "

The benefit performance itself was a resounding success. Each year from 1934 to 1939, the event filled the 3,300-seat building with many of New York City's most influential people. From September until just after Christmas, Keller devoted long hours working with various committees, preparing a program with first-class ads and assigning seats. On the night of the great occasion, Keller positioned himself at the entrance of the opera house to greet each incoming person. The music itself was largely lost on him, for he was busy moving from one section to another to thank his principal benefactors.

Aside from raising about $7,000 a year, after expenses, for Maryknoll's mission work, the annual benefit generated a great deal of publicity and good will for the still-struggling society. On some occasions, Keller had to fill the house by donating unsold seats to Maryknollers and other friends. One year, a group of missioners just back from China came to the Met, only to walk out at the intermission. Instead of returning, they made for Downey's Steak House for a slice of prime ribs and a couple of beers. "The voice of culture" was not for them.

Keller urged his priest-assistants to spend 80 percent of their time talking to students on the secondary and college level; although many of them preferred to devote their efforts to children on the elementary level, who were not so demanding. Keller himself spoke in about thirty-five schools a year. He gradually increased his tempo until in 1937 he gave talks in fifty-eight schools, which just about covered every Catholic institution of its kind in the archdiocese. To increase Maryknoll's visibility, he even attended a number of graduations, though he found them "boring."

Keller's school talks had a special appeal to youth, for he held out to them the challenge of self-sacrifice in an up-to-date manner. His delivery was laced with contemporary terms and references, yet his message was, in his words, "as old as the hills." He repeatedly stressed that the Catholic Church was truly itself only when it was pushing out the frontiers by proclaiming the Gospel of forgiveness and ministering to the needs of suffering humanity. He was instrumental in many religious vocations, but more than that, he left an indelible impression on his hearers that they could and should do something constructive with their lives. It was the Christopher message long before he started the actual Christopher organization.

School talks were demanding, but calling on pastors to persuade them to sign up Maryknollers for church dates was probably the hardest part of any promoter's existence. Keller compiled an enviable record, but he had more than a few turn-downs. One of his hardest-won victories was over a pastor in Stamford, Connecticut, whom he stopped in to see eight times over a two-year period. Either the pastor wasn't home or the answer was no. Keller's diary then recorded: "Lo and behold, the poor old pastor, so sick of seeing me, finally breaks down and gives just the Sunday we want. Hope he doesn't get a relapse." He didn't.

On other occasions, Keller wasn't so fortunate. One evening he drove to churches in Mamaroneck, Larchmont, and New Rochelle, in the northern suburbs of New York City . . . "without even one date to show that the gasoline wasn't wasted." He philosophized: "Openings are not all wrapped up in cellophane for us to pick up and carry off." At one point Keller devised a plan to catch pastors at home, which they often were not. He picked November 1, the Feast of All Saints and a holy day of obligation, to stop in at rectories in Manhattan. With full Mass schedules to accommodate the people, surely they would be on the job. Keller called in on six pastors—from 12th Street to 165th Street—and found none at home.

Sometimes a promoter was better off when the boss wasn't in. In one Brooklyn church, Keller was ushered out as quickly as he came in. "At such moments," he commented, "one's motives for wanting to be in China are not altogether Grade A." On the same rainy night, he drove to a second church where the housekeeper, after considerable delay, came back with the unconvincing story that the pastor wasn't in—not to him anyway. At a third church, he was put off for six months. Next day, he was out along the Hudson River route looking for pastors. Again, no success. "No runs, no errors," was his conclusion.

"It is more difficult to get dates in New York," he wrote in his diary, "because of hard times and many appeals, but particularly because it is so difficult to find pastors at home. Last week we went to ten churches and found only one or two at home. After they saw us, they were sorry they weren't out, too!"

One of the more creative pastors lived in Greenwich, Connecticut, a wealthy parish. Not only was he "out," but he had a sign placed where all would-be solicitors could see it. The comprehensiveness of his edict was summed up in the concluding words: "And this means everybody collecting, whether they be from the East, West, North or South." Keller's comment: "But we may be able to get him yet." And he did.

Some pastors just needed a little psychology, like the one at St. Gregory's in Manhattan. Father O'Donnell, in Keller's words, "did everything but shove me down the chimney when I first met him." Then the good priest complained about his $400,000 debt and the large number of poor people in his parish. Keller, of course, was thinking of the rich people in the same parish. When O'Donnell had blown off all his steam, with Keller reacting sympathetically, there was a moment of silence. Being a good-hearted man, the pastor relented and allowed the Maryknoller to preach at all the Masses.

There were also "good guys," like Father Coggin of Rye, another parish in a northern suburb, who always welcomed Maryknoll appeals, despite his $500,000 debt. Parishes conducted by religious orders, such as the Jesuits, were usually accommodating. These groups had foreign missionaries of their own and knew all about the good work of Maryknollers, as well as the difficulties of fund-raising.

Even Keller's patience was tested to the limit one Sunday in 1934 at Our Savior's, a working-class parish in the Bronx. At each Mass, the pastor preached for twelve minutes about the "poor giving habits" of his people. That left Keller with all of two minutes to talk about the missions. To make matters worse, it was a desperately hot day and three other collections preceded the one for Maryknoll. Despite everything, the long-suffering parishioners contributed $258 in cash, 190 subscribed to *The Field Afar*, and twenty-nine signed up as sponsors.

It was becoming clear to Keller that the "mission" of the Church was much bigger than Maryknoll. With a conviction that he felt but could not prove, the realization grew in Keller that his ultimate work would be to kindle that personal sense of mission in each individual into a flame in many hearts.

But this conviction would have to take a back seat for the next four years, for Keller was about to embark on the most frustrating period of his life. He would learn much about the human side of the Church during those years, and find his optimism severely tried.

•6•

The Propagation
of the Faith

*"The explanation of why the average American Catholic is
not mission-minded narrows down to the national central
office. . . . It must be geared up considerably to meet what
necessity demands if the Catholics of the country are to have
a real knowledge of why and how to spread their faith."*
James Keller

In 1822, Pauline Jaricot, a French laywoman, started the Society
for the Propagation of the Faith (SPF) in Lyon. Her purpose was
to provide financial support for Catholic missionaries throughout
the world. These missionaries had followed in the wake of European
colonial expansion in many parts of Asia and Africa. The SPF
helped the mission societies to spread the Gospel, but the organization's major contribution was to the education of indigenous seminarians and catechists who formed local churches in mission areas.

The United States was considered a mission territory until 1908.
As a sign that the Church in the United States was prepared to
support itself and take on a more active role in foreign mission
work, a branch of the SPF was established in 1897 in Boston, where
Archbishop John Williams vigorously supported it. In 1903, the
newly appointed archdiocesan director of the society, Father James
Anthony Walsh, immersed himself so deeply in the work that he
eventually became the cofounder of the nation's first American
Catholic mission society—Maryknoll.

A National Office for the SPF was set up in New York to co-
ordinate the activities of local directors in the country's 103 arch-

dioceses and dioceses. But by the late 1920s, the National Office, headed by Monsignor William Quinn, a priest from Omaha, Nebraska, had fallen into a comfortable rut. No one was more aware of this than James Anthony Walsh, who expressed his concern to Archbishop John T. McNicholas of Cincinnati, a powerful proponent of the missionary movement. Their distress was shared by Archbishop Amleto Cicognani who, as Apostolic Delegate to the United States, was the personal representative of the Pope to the American Catholic hierarchy.

As a confidant of Walsh, James Keller was only too aware of the sorry state of the National Office. In 1933, with Walsh's encouragement, Keller held several conversations with Quinn and what he learned served to confirm his conviction that something positive had to be done.

Keller discovered that donations to the Propagation of the Faith from the United States had been stagnant for a number of years. In addition, much of its income came from investments—the result of large donations made years before—and its stock portfolio was subject to no outside controls. Quinn was an affable man with little vision or sense of organization who had apparently found a pleasant niche for himself and enjoyed the social contacts his position afforded. His assistant, Father Hubert Campo of Lincoln, Nebraska, moved at an even slower pace, if that were possible. Campo's main function at the National Office seemed to be to collect cancelled stamps from elementary schools, the sale of which benefited the missions to the tune of about $450 in a good year. Except for a few active centers such as Boston, Detroit, and Milwaukee, the SPF in the United States was little more than a paper organization.

The meetings with Quinn sent Keller's brain whirring. Although he had his hands full raising money for Maryknoll, Keller devised a plan for "revamping the whole national policy" of the National Office of the SPF. It involved close personal contact with all diocesan directors, better organization of the annual Mission Sunday (the third Sunday of October) collection in the churches of each diocese, and more effective collaboration with missionary orders, such as Maryknoll, the Jesuits, and the Franciscans. Keller sent his plan to Walsh, McNicholas, and Considine, confiding to Considine that McNicholas was "vitally interested and . . . the only chance to get action is through him." Keller's idea of action was to have a "live-wire priest," preferably one from a missionary society, assigned to the National Office to get things moving again.

McNicholas was of the same mind, and in 1934 asked Walsh if Keller could be made available for the work on a temporary, part-time basis. Walsh decided to take the matter to the Apostolic Delegate. He and Keller traveled to Washington in June of that year for the meeting with Cicognani, whose concurrence was vital. As Keller recalled the meeting:

> The Delegate asked Bishop Walsh [Maryknoll's superior had been consecrated bishop the year before] if he could help by allowing me to assist Monsignor Quinn. He is writing the latter and suggesting that he communicate with Bishop Walsh on Sunday in regard to final arrangements.

Quinn agreed to take on Keller as a temporary assistant, but to everyone's later discomfort, the latter's duties were vaguely defined. Nevertheless, Keller was elated. He expressed confidence that he could be of help to the monsignor without allowing his Maryknoll duties to suffer. In this he was mistaken. And he was mistaken, too, if he thought that Quinn would give him a free hand to make the kind of changes that were thought necessary. Only a month after he took on his new assignment, Keller wrote with disappointment to Considine:

> The Delegate has sized up Msgr. Quinn in exactly the same way that I have. He said that I should stay at the National Office no matter what happens. He said he realized how difficult it was for me, but to put up with it, for the sake of the Cause, until some relief comes.

Relief was a long time coming—three years, to be exact. Meanwhile, Keller did as much as he could. He was fortunate to have a place to live at the National Office, for Julia Ward, who owned the building in which Keller lived and worked on 48th Street, was forced to sell it. Keller would have been out on the street but for the fact that there were living quarters for him at the SPF office.

Despite Quinn's resistance to change, Keller managed to redesign

Catholic Missions, the SPF's monthly magazine, and in doing so he patterned its format after *Pictorial California*, a lively travel magazine from his home state. To brighten the look of the publication, he purchased photos from commercial distributors and from Fides, a worldwide mission news and photo service that had been started by Considine in Rome. Bishops and diocesan directors were delighted with the "new look" of *Catholic Missions*. This initial success gave Keller enough leeway to throw out the dusty old calendar that the SPF sent to contributors and to replace it with a much more contemporary one—at half the cost. In the calendar's first year, 500,000 copies were distributed.

It was during his assignment to the Propagation of the Faith that Keller began to see the advantages of a new communications medium—radio—which he would use so effectively in later years. He plotted and planned with Considine to arrange for the Pope to make an English-language radio broadcast to the people of the United States on Mission Sunday. It was to have had a nationwide hook-up over the National Broadcasting Company, whose vice-president, Franklin Dunham, was years later to set up the Vatican Radio in Rome. As it turned out, Pope Pius XI was kept in the dark concerning the offer, because Vatican bureaucrats were too blind to see the value in what would have been an excellent bit of publicity for the Church. Keller and Considine had to settle for a "hearts and flowers" statement by an Italian cardinal and a short address by an American bishop. It had to be left to future pontiffs to make the optimal use of the broadcast media.

In a cost-cutting effort, Keller prevailed upon Quinn to reduce staff salaries at the National Office by 10 percent. He himself received no compensation for his work. He did all he could to reduce food bills, which, however, continued to be high even when most of the priest-residents were away. Keller told Considine: "I'm not a crank on economy, but it does hurt to see money going like that which maybe some poor soul has given at a sacrifice and which would mean a tremendous help to some struggling missioner." Keller also set a much-needed example for the staff by showing up for work promptly at 9 A.M.

Despite the headway he was making, Keller knew that Quinn viewed him with suspicion. "Monsignor Quinn is very kind and cordial," he told Walsh, "but I am not 'taken in' by it." Quinn shook off his façade of friendliness when Keller recommended that the National Office employ the services of an accountant. Like many Catholic parishes, and even dioceses at that time, the National Office was run with scarcely any financial controls or accountability. Keller saw this sloppy procedure as a potential powderkeg. So did Walsh, McNicholas, and several of the diocesan directors. Keller met with a predictable response:

> He [Quinn] almost hit the ceiling . . . and demanded quite indignantly why there was any necessity for it. With all the poise of a smoker of Murads [a popular cigarette], I replied that it was needed for the same reason that any simple organization did it.

If relations with Quinn were tense, Campo's return from a two-month vacation in Europe made Keller's life nearly unbearable. The modest concessions for improvement that Keller had wrested from Quinn were suddenly reversed once the influential Campo was on the scene. So disturbed was Keller that he launched into an uncharacteristic attack on Campo in a confidential memo to Quinn:

> It is commonly known that he lacks personality, tact, a practical sense of mission values and that he is cold, stubborn, critical, pessimistic and either doesn't see how, cannot, or doesn't want to improve his touch with the common mind. He has offended many Directors by his abrupt manner with them.

Coming from the man who believed in lighting candles instead of cursing the darkness, this was quite an explosion. In fact, after conferring with McNicholas, Keller decided not to waste his time sending the memo to Quinn. McNicholas, an astute student of human nature, advised Keller that Quinn "can no more change his mental processes than he can change the shape of his head."

McNicholas told Keller that the removal of Quinn at this point would embarrass the Holy See. He wrote:

> I am sure you evaluate the difficulties of Monsignor Quinn's superiors. He cannot be charged with faults that are of his

making. He simply lacks gifts, which means that he never was qualified for his present position. Yet representations were made which induced Rome to make him a Prelate [a Monsignor is considered a prelate] and, later a Protonotary. This means that the Holy See has publicly expressed confidence in him. His position cannot now be reversed, nor can he be gracefully demoted, unless for reasons of health or some other grave cause. I think a year's leave of absence would be an excellent temporary solution.

By this time Quinn wanted to get rid of Keller, but McNicholas and Cicognani wanted him to remain. To clarify the matter, Walsh wrote to Quinn:

> I know that you have expressed to others your dissatisfaction with Father Keller, and I am asking myself why you did not bring your complaint directly to me.
>
> When at your request we loaned Father Keller to you, it was with an honest purpose to help you reorganize the important work of which you are the responsible head. You saw in Father Keller the prospect of a precious aid, and you were right; I consider his services invaluable.
>
> If you now wish to dispense with them, I shall be at Maryknoll on Tuesday, September 25—[1934]—preferably after 3:00 P.M.—and ready to talk over the situation.

When the meeting took place, Quinn asked for Keller's removal. Walsh countered that the request be put in writing. Quinn did so in a letter dated September 26, 1934: "In view of all the circumstances, I think it advisable if Father Keller would withdraw as Assistant National Director as of November first."

But Quinn was not let off the hook so easily. Keller, who was learning fast, told the monsignor that the final decision would have to be made by the Apostolic Delegate himself. Perhaps not wishing to rock the boat with Cicognani, Quinn backed off. Matters were at a stalemate.

On the publicity front, however, Keller was putting the Propagation of the Faith on the map. He sent a copy of *Catholic Missions* to Henry Luce, publisher of *Time* magazine, and received this reply (10/3/34):

Permit me, as the son of a Protestant missionary, to congratulate you most heartily on your Missions Roto Magazine. The selection of pictures has clearly been done by a real editor. And the value you give each one by printing it alone on a page is notable. I do not recall ever having seen a more striking mission document.

In its edition of October 10, 1934, *Time* ran nearly two columns on the magazine put out by "the boyish young priest named Rev. James G. Keller." The article pointed out: "Few will be aware that it is not only the first religious picture magazine but also the biggest job of rotogravure ever done in the U.S.—2,843,000 copies of the first issue." Also on the bright side was the fact that returns from the Mission Sunday collection were rising. Detroit and Milwaukee had doubled their previous year's totals.

Meanwhile, Campo was removed from his post and departed to his home diocese of Lincoln, Nebraska. Three members of the Catholic hierarchy—Cardinal Patrick Hayes of New York, Bishop Joseph Ritter of Indianapolis, and Bishop Francis P. Keogh of Providence—were appointed to a committee to reorganize the National Office. As Keller described their takeover:

> They came over in battle formation for an official call on Monsignor Quinn last week and had him on the carpet for some time. Later in the day, the Cardinal had me come over to his residence and tell the trio what was what. They were all very nice to me. The Delegate wants to put everything entirely in the hands of the Bishops, and this is wise, so there will be no comeback on him.

Encouraged by this turn of events, Keller mounted a nationwide drive to enroll one million members at $1 per year, increased the circulation of *Catholic Missions*, wrote weekly news notes to the directors, and publicized the SPF in the diocesan and daily press. He also made personal visits to diocesan directors. In one three-week swing in late summer 1935, he touched base with nearly thirty of them in the South and the West. One of the main purposes of these visits was to ask them to make recommendations for improving the public relations activities of the National Office. In that way, Keller felt, the impetus for improvements would not come from him alone. "I am anxious to give my best efforts to strengthening the Propagation of the Faith," he wrote, "and then to fade out of the picture as soon as someone else is found to pick up my portion of the work and carry on."

With Considine back at Maryknoll as Director of Propaganda, Keller's correspondent in Rome was Father Edward McGurkin. McGurkin praised Keller for the improvements in *Catholic Missions*, but felt some of the stylistic changes he made were a bit artificial. He also lamented the many "sob stories" in the magazine. In reply, Keller wrote:

> We acknowledge gratefully your advice on the "sob stories." I came to the conclusion about seven-and-a-half years ago that most people are 98 percent sentimental and about two percent logical, so if they want sob stories, sob stories we will give them. How to get the stories is the problem, as we are bound to get a lot that are a bit messy, and not worthwhile—but we shall follow your instructions.

Quinn was given a three-month leave of absence early in 1936, and with the monsignor out of the picture, Keller had even more freedom of movement. As he described one meeting with the bishops' committee in May 1936:

> We had the big meeting here and things came off much better than I expected. I gave the biggest fight talk of my life to the Board of Directors, and did everything but tell them they would all go to blazes if they didn't take more interest in building up this work from an income of $600,000 or $700,000 a year to something like $2,000,000. I talked almost without stopping for two hours. It must have made an impression, because they all admitted that they had really gotten the idea of the purpose of the National Office after I had given my song-and-dance.

During this period of intense activity, the Maryknoll Society, in April 1936, lost its cofounder, James Anthony Walsh. It was an especially heavy blow to Keller, who had come to look upon Walsh as a father-figure, an advisor, and a source of encouragement. With the death of the cofounder, Keller entered a ten-year period in which the administration at Maryknoll regarded him with a distinct coolness. Maryknoll's new superior general was yet another Walsh—James Edward Walsh—the same priest who formed part of the society's first mission group that went to China in 1918, and he regarded Keller's activities more cautiously than had his predecessor.

Keller kept trying to find a graceful exit from his SPF activities. In November 1936, he wrote to the new superior general:

> On the 22nd of next month, I shall have been at the National Office just two-and-a-half years. Inasmuch as the reorganization has been practically completed, it seems quite in order that I should pass in my resignation as National Secretary and Director of Promotion. I am prompted in this also by the fact that . . . the needs of Maryknoll are steadily growing more serious, and that I have a definite obligation in regard to them.

Keller wrote to Monsignor Thomas McDonnell, Acting National Director, setting the date for his resignation, but added that he would stay until a replacement could be found. That took another year.

Keller's departure from the National Office was set for the end of 1937. To mark the occasion, a testimonial luncheon was held in his honor. In the course of a speech thanking Keller for his three-and-a-half years of uncompensated service, McDonnell handed the Maryknoller a check for $1,000. Although it was presented in all good faith, Keller immediately saw unintended complications if he accepted it. In an era of high unemployment and deflated currency, Keller felt that $1,000 for Maryknoll would be regarded as a very large amount of money, and that the society would be criticized for doing "pretty well" for itself, even though the sum was a pittance in view of his forty-two months' work. Keller also realized that had he been free to pursue the interests of Maryknoll, he could have raised as much as $150,000 and brought in many more vocational prospects for his society.

As thoughts like these rushed through his head, Keller took a chance. At the risk of offending the assembled SPF officials and well-wishers, he refused the check, expressing his gratitude but explaining that Maryknoll wished no reimbursement. Murmurs of surprise swept the table, but his unexpected action was favorably received.

Back at Maryknoll headquarters, James E. Walsh was not so sure that Keller had acted wisely. Walsh feared that hurt feelings would arise from the refusal. Eventually, a face-saving compromise was reached, whereby the money went to Joe Sweeney's leper colony in China. On this amicable note, the often stormy relationship between Keller and the National Office came to an end. William Quinn never returned from his extended leave of absence, and he died in 1938.

It would be no exaggeration to say that Keller's participation in the affairs of the SPF saved the organization from oblivion. He reanimated the flagging spirits of its hard-pressed diocesan directors, popularized the cause of the missions by modernizing *Catholic Missions*, increased income, and introduced strict financial controls. He prepared the way for the steady growth of the SPF under McDonnell until Bishop Fulton J. Sheen became its national director in 1950. Although it was Sheen who led the Propagation of the Faith into its "glory days" through his writings and nationwide television programs, without Keller there may not have been a viable organization for Sheen to inherit.

As far as Maryknoll was concerned, Keller returned to full-time work none too soon. With growing numbers of missioners to maintain in war-torn China, the society's financial condition remained precarious.

• 7 •

People and Places

*"My only regret about them [the rich] is that they don't
realize how much more fun they could get out of life if they
thought less about themselves and more about the 99.9% of
humanity who have so little of what is theirs."*

James Keller

Keller's experience with the Propagation of the Faith extended his
horizons, for it led him out of the narrow circle of Maryknoll and
its supporters, putting him in closer touch with many members of
the American Catholic hierarchy. His battles with Quinn and Campo
also toughened him for future campaigns.

Another broadening influence on Keller during the thirties was
foreign travel. In 1933 he journeyed to Rome as the sole Maryknoll
traveling companion of James Anthony Walsh, who was conse-
crated bishop on June 29, the Society's twenty-second anniversary.
Keller's most lasting impression in Italy was of the early Christian
martyrs, who never failed to inspire him. He reflected often on
how these "Christophers" shed their blood in bearing witness to
Christ. Most of them were lay people, and they needed no formal
ecclesiastical mandate to speak and act as they did. It was the natural
consequence of their faith.

Keller's second trip was a cruise in 1937 to South America, a
rest as much as anything else, for Keller was near exhaustion from
overwork. Both trips were eye-openers to a man so singlemindedly
dedicated to his immediate objectives that he ran the risk of becoming too one-dimensional.

The cruise on the *Aquitania*, a luxury liner, was taken under doctor's orders to get all the sunshine and rest he could. With a free pass from the Cunard Line, the thirty-seven-year-old priest put in at such ports as Barbados, Trinidad, Caracas, Rio de Janeiro, Montevideo, and Buenos Aires. Instructed by his physician not even to do any serious reading, Keller took full advantage of the ship's two outdoor swimming pools, deck tennis facilities, and other shipboard sports. Most important, he got plenty of sleep—a relaxation he could never get enough of all his life.

Keller got to know most of the 570 passengers on this "millionaire's cruise," as well as many of the crew members who, in his words, "didn't get all the spiritual attention they deserve." Among the prominent names on the passenger list were Dr. Jacob Schurman, former president of Cornell University and Ambassador to Germany, the widow of Andrew Carnegie, and the Frederick Weyerhaeusers, who owned extensive lumber interests. Keller found, to his satisfaction, that his fellow passengers were educated, cultured, and conservative. "While it is true that they spend so much time, thought and money on their own comfort and ease," he observed, "yet I hesitate to criticize them for I'd probably do worse if I were in the same circumstances." Because he knew and liked many rich people, Keller found it hard to be hostile to them, even though their antiunion policies oppressed working-class people whom he cared for no less warmly. Unlike some clerics who more or less "fell in" with the attitudes of the wealthy, Keller believed in trying to persuade them to a greater sense of social justice. The way of confrontation was not his.

Of the various places Keller visited, Rio made the greatest impression on him—"a dream city that cannot be quickly forgotten." On the South American tour as a whole, Keller summed it up in his usual cheerful way: "A free ticket, a grand boat, a wonderful trip, marvelous friends, plenty of rest, gorgeous weather, many spiritual consolations and, on top of it all, a few thousand dollars more for the missions. Well, I am deeply grateful to the good Lord."

Matters that were strictly related to Maryknoll could not absorb all his thoughts and energies. The Franciscan Sisters of Mary asked Keller to give them some pointers on obtaining funds for their sanatorium for children in Roslyn, New York. He suggested a direct mail approach to wealthy non-Catholics on Long Island. They followed his advice, but sixty-three letters produced nothing. "They decided to send a 64th with misgivings," he wrote. "But it did the trick, for it went to a Presbyterian who was impressed by it and is now giving them $100,000 for the new building. . . . They need about $50,000 more for equipment and so I helped them as best I could regarding stationery, printing and even helped them frame another letter and bulletin. Might as well help wherever we can."

A problem to which Keller devoted some of his time was the depiction of sex and violence in motion pictures, which was growing increasingly explicit. In a letter to a friend, Mrs. August Belmont, Keller wrote (3/23/34):

> For the past five years I have closely watched the trend in movies both here . . . and in Hollywood. I was in contact with several producers, actors and actresses, and I was at last convinced of the truth of what George Cohan once said to the effect that the only way to get a clean slate is to "hit the box-office."

The "box-office" approach was taken up by Archbishop Mc-Nicholas, head of the National Catholic Office for Motion Pictures. With the help of Martin Quigley, publisher of *Motion Picture Herald*, and Jesuits Daniel Lord and Fitzgeorge Dineen, the prelate set up the Legion of Decency. With the failure of Hollywood's self-regulatory system (the Hays Office, set up in 1922), the Legion confronted the flood of "objectionable" movies by asking Catholics to take a pledge once a year during Mass not to patronize such films. Keller played a peripheral role in the planning that led to the establishment of the Legion of Decency, chiefly through consultations with McNicholas, who asked him to handle national publicity for the pledge. Keller did so, but probably with some reluctance, for he considered "censorships, condemnations, protests, etc.," to have limited value. He preferred the positive approach, which he adopted years later through the creation of the Christopher Awards. In this outlook, Keller was in agreement with George Shuster, editor of *Commonweal*, a lay-edited Catholic weekly, who had written with some foresight (*Commonweal*, 2/2/27):

> Catholics in this country can kill a motion picture which is offensive to their religious (or social) convictions—but they cannot and do not accomplish anything to render the art of the

cinema less stupidly sentimental and more worthy of citizens come to the age of reason.

As Keller's interests widened, his ties to Maryknoll grew somewhat weaker. With the death of James Anthony Walsh in the spring of 1936, Keller not only lost a dear friend but much of his influence on Maryknoll policy. Like McNicholas, Walsh had leaned on Keller for advice. It is likely that the Maryknoll superior would have liked to appoint Keller to a position on the Society's governing Council, as vacancies occurred, but other Council members (particularly James Drought and Patrick Byrne) dissuaded him, feeling that Keller had too much influence on Walsh as it was. According to Father John McConnell, now in retirement in Los Altos, California, "I'm quite sure he [Walsh] wanted Keller. And Drought didn't want him because he felt that Keller would supplant him."[1]

The death of James Anthony Walsh left Maryknoll without a superior general. A meeting of delegates to choose a successor and four assistants to the superior general was held in Hong Kong in 1936. John Considine attended this meeting (called a General Chapter), while Keller filled in as acting director of propaganda. Charles McCarthy, now recovered from his illnesses and working with Considine at Maryknoll, New York, seems to have taken offense at being passed over in favor of Keller. McCarthy informed Keller in a memo that is hard to take at face value: ". . . it would be an injustice to expect you to do the work at Maryknoll which the Council has assigned to you and . . . consequently I have assumed all responsibility for propaganda, publicity, *Field Afar* and office work."

James Edward Walsh, as we have seen, was chosen to be Maryknoll's second superior, a position he held from 1936 to 1946. He respected Keller for his accomplishments, but was much more cautious by nature that the other Walsh. Some idea of how Keller fit into his administration can be gleaned from this letter the new superior wrote Keller shortly after his election (October 1936):

> I need not remind you that through you, more than through any of the rest of us, Maryknoll will be known and judged around the country. You are our façade. I feel confident that you will always edify, that you will implant love for Maryknoll

and the missions in the hearts of tens of thousands. I think you should bear particularly in mind your special task of winning the priests.

To James E. Walsh, a man who chose his words carefully, Keller was to be Maryknoll's "front man," or façade. There was no indication that Keller would have a hand in the development of policy, only its implementation.

Was Keller drifting from Maryknoll, or at least chafing at the routine of promotion work? If so, it was probably not conscious. But the question returns: could a conscientious priest with such unusual talents remain content with the necessarily superficial contacts with people that promotion work called for? As one who kept abreast of news of economic depression, labor strife, and international tensions, Keller must have felt at times that his work for Maryknoll offered as yet unrealized opportunities for involvement in the great issues that troubled the world. In a letter written October 18, 1945, Keller dated his interest in starting the Christophers to this period. He wrote to James E. Walsh:

> It had long been my hope that Maryknoll would be able to take some active interest in the enormous work to be done in this country in saving the Christian tradition that seems to be fast disintegrating with the breakdown of Protestantism. . . . Nearly seven years ago, it occurred to me to volunteer for this phase of the work that seemed even at that time so important. But in view of my limitations and because I felt serious obligations to Maryknoll, I put aside the thought.

Keller's words reflect a common Catholic attitude that was well summarized in a statement by a Jesuit historian who wrote of the "desolating spectacle of human degeneration, of debasement of the arts, of letters, and of education, and the indescribable confusion of thought—indeed, the collapse of civilization."[2]

This gloomy assessment of what was happening outside the Catholic Church was shared by most Catholics. The response of church leaders was to keep their people safe in their own religious ghetto, impervious to the influences of modern thought, or openly hostile to it. Between 1919 and the early 1950s, no less than fifteen—and possibly more—Catholic organizations were founded to parallel existing groups. These interacted only slightly with their secular counterparts, and suspicion between the two camps was mutual. In 1944, for example, the distinguished professor of history at Columbia University, Carlton J. H. Hayes, a Catholic, ran into stiff opposition when his name was proposed for the presidency of the American Historical Association. How, after all, could a Catholic be an honest historian? As it turned out, Hayes was elected, but other groups continued to view each other nervously.

Keller felt that the purely defensive stance was a futile one. He knew that most Catholics were practically untouched by these special organizations set up for their protection, and that his coreligionists paid little heed to Catholic diocesan newspapers and periodicals. He favored the involvement of Catholics in the secular world, as in the case of Neil McNeil, an editor of the *New York Times*, who was responsible for that paper's decision to print the full text of papal encyclicals; or later that of John Delaney, an editor at Doubleday, who brought out a line of books (Image Books) that proved that general publishers could sell religious books to a large Catholic audience. Keller never spoke disparagingly of Catholic "ghetto tactics," but his strategy was one of penetration, not withdrawal.

As William M. Halsey points out: "From World War I and continuing into the 1950s, their [Catholics'] isolation from contemporary literary currents was a very conspicuous element of American Catholic culture."[3] Halsey argues persuasively that the Catholic body was practically the sole repository of an older tradition of American optimism, belief in a natural moral law, and a rational approach to the ambiguities of politics, ethics, and economics. Arrayed against them were the forces of pragmatism in public life, skepticism in literature, positivism in philosophy and relativism in law and morality.

Although most of Keller's writings date from the 1940s and 1950s, his thought was formed in the thirties. He held firmly to the prevailing concept of a harmonious, ordered universe, a concept endorsed by the revival of the philosophy of St. Thomas Aquinas. In this, he shared the view of such Catholic controversialists as Father James Gillis of *The Catholic World*, Fulton J. Sheen, and such British literary lights as G. K. Chesterton and Hillaire Belloc. Keller left it to others to point out where the modern world was wrong.

Most of his literary output was an attempt to win over non-Catholics to those aspects of Catholic teaching that were commonly held by most Americans in previous centuries. He paid no attention to the negative aspects of Catholicism, such as the Inquisition, the Galileo affair, abuses that led to the Reformation, or the nineteenth-century popes' opposition to modern ideas of democracy. An Americanist in the tradition of Archbishops Hughes, Ireland, and Gibbons, he stressed that the political constitution of the United States was in harmony with Catholic tradition. To him, as to these predecessors, it was almost as though God spoke through the "inalienable rights" doctrine contained in the Declaration of Independence as assuredly as he did through the New Testament.

Keller's dedication to the concept of individual rights emerges from an account he left of a meeting in 1937 with the Abbé le Maitre, a French intellectual who worked for a time with Albert Einstein at Princeton University. Keller wrote to James E. Walsh (11/2/43) about the meeting which had taken place about six years earlier:

> I was particularly impressed when he [Le Maitre] said that the one factor that had contributed more than anything else in winning sympathy for Hitler from the German people was that he reduced his whole philosophy to four or five basic ideas, and kept repeating them over and over again. The Abbé said that the Catholic Church in Europe was in for a great deal of trouble if it didn't adopt a similar formula for emphasizing over and over again the four or five great fundamentals of Christianity.

Among these fundamentals, Keller placed stress in the same letter on one above all:

> Probably the reason why I stress the sacredness of the individual is because that idea has done more than anything else to keep up any devotion I have as a priest and whatever little enthusiasm I may put into our work. It has also been the most powerful idea I have found in winning vocations and supporters, and in drawing irreligious people to a sense of religion, for it seems to open the way, more easily than anything else, to an understanding of the love of God and of man. . . .

His stress on the individual is the key to Keller's subsequent activity. It was not uniquely Catholic, but it was part of his church's body of doctrine. Other social movements of the time, such as Catholic Action, stressed the doctrine of the Mystical Body of Christ. This movement, which was strongly encouraged by Pope Pius XI (1919–1939), was comprised of such elite groups as the Young Christian Students, Young Christian Workers, the Newman Club Federation (in colleges), and the Christian Family Movement. Catholic Action, which was defined as the "participation of the laity in the apostolate of the hierarchy," Keller felt, was too rigidly structured for the average American. Harking back to the early Christians whose monuments had left such an impression on him in Rome, Keller didn't think people had to sit around waiting for an "episcopal mandate." Keller never publicly took issue with Catholic Action, with its repeated stress on "spiritual formation." He simply ignored it, which was galling to many Catholic Actionists.

Keller's outlook was also shaped by the experience of Maryknoll missioners in China and elsewhere, who could not enter directly into politics. Keller felt that direct political action, like that of Father Charles Coughlin (who fielded a slate of candidates in the presidential election of 1936), was not the province of a priest. He preferred to appeal directly to the Catholic laity—and others of "good will"—to find their own ways of bringing about social and political change. He would stick to the "four or five fundamentals." Another tactic of Keller's, following that of his fellow missionaries, was to seek, directly or indirectly, the conversion of non-Catholics to Catholicism. In his lifetime, he was quietly responsible for many such conversions, though he never kept any record of them. This approach he gradually deemphasized as a widespread means for social change. If an idea didn't work, his custom was to discard it.

Keller never believed that his approach to "modern paganism" was the only one, though he obviously thought it was the best one for many people. His attitude received some confirmation years later (1963) from one of the church's leading theologians, Karl Rahner, S.J., who wrote in his book, *The Christian Commitment*:

> Christians *as such* do not have any ready-made concrete program for the conduct of the State, or of culture, or of economics and in fact they *cannot* have one. . . . It is now coming to be grad-

ually clear that the gap between universal Christian principles and the putting of them into practice in any one of a number of possible forms is a gap as wide as the possibilities now opening before us.[4]

Keller's openness can be seen in his attitude toward Dorothy Day, once a left-wing journalist and later a founder of the Catholic Worker movement. The two met in 1937 at the home of J. Peter Grace, who was to become head of the steamship company and the multinational corporation that bears his name. Deeply moved by Dorothy Day's sincerity and charity, Keller wrote to Mc-Nicholas (2/1/37):

> I have had a most interesting chat with Miss Dorothy Day, who is so closely identified with the Catholic Worker movement. While she is not 100% in everything [possibly a reference to her pacifism and strong criticism of capitalism], yet I believe that she is basically very sound, especially when she says that the only effective way to beat Communists is by showing in a practical way the love and solicitude of Christ, and particularly by means of the corporal works of mercy. She gave many other pointers, too, that rang true, and which could be put into practice very easily in any parish.

In her autobiography, *The Long Loneliness*,[5] Dorothy Day told the story from her perspective:

> Father James G. Keller, head of the Christopher Movement [an anachronism, since this was 1937], called me one day and said that Archbishop McNicholas would like to talk to me, so I took a train to Cincinnati. . . . On that happy occasion when I enjoyed the day with the Archbishop, who, like so many others, lived in poverty in the midst of wealth, Father Keller and I listened to him read a pastoral letter he had just written. It was about the condition of capital and labor, and I felt it was a noble piece of writing. But Father Keller thought the archbishop was a trifle harsh to the rich.

Keller submitted to McNicholas a plan for helping the poor through grass-roots parish action "as the result of talks with Monsignor

Fulton Sheen, Father John Considine and Miss Dorothy Day in the last two days." Though McNicholas approved of it, such was the independence of Catholic dioceses that it stood little chance of nationwide approval. Keller and Miss Day went their separate ways after 1937, though each held the other in high regard. What did endure was McNicholas' interest in the Catholic Worker movement. He and Dorothy Day were to have their differences, but the prelate helped the Catholic Worker in financial and other ways. He sent her his special blessing years later when he was dying.

Keller kept in close touch with the Grace family. Peter and his brother Michael were grateful to Keller for the part he played in their mother's deathbed conversion to the Catholic faith. Both became generous supporters of Maryknoll and afterward the Christophers—as did their younger brother, Charles. Years later, when the three brothers had a falling out, Keller worked behind the scenes to effect a reconciliation by talking with their wives.

Friendship with the Graces brought Keller into contact with a new set of friends, with whom he spent time in the summer months of 1940. At the family's summer retreat in Northeast Harbor, Maine, Keller stayed up late with various notables explaining the work of Catholic missionaries. Among them were Mrs. Marshall Field, Mrs. Nicholas Longworth, and Sonia Stokowski, daughter of the conductor. In an ecumenical encounter, he received a compliment on *The Field Afar* from Dr. McCracken, a high official of the Presbyterian Church. Despite the late hours he kept, Keller often had to arise at 6 A.M. to drive several miles to the local church to offer weekday Mass. "One can always make up lost sleep later!" he said bravely, but he could never seem to get enough.

Father Fitzpatrick, pastor of the Seal Harbor church, was especially gracious to the visiting Maryknoller. This is noteworthy because, as pastor of an impoverished year-round congregation, he might have resented Keller for "horning in" on his affluent summer parishioners. Instead, Fitzpatrick allowed Keller to preach on Sunday and to distribute sponsor cards, and in return, out of deference to the pastor, Keller did not take up a collection. When Peter and Michael Grace learned of their pastor's generosity, they sent him $500.

Another prominent Catholic family—the Joseph P. Kennedys—played host to Keller in the summer of 1940. Their oldest daughter,

Kathleen, invited the Maryknoller to talk to a group of her friends at Hyannis, Massachusetts. Many discussions followed in the next few days about religion and Maryknoll's work in the world. "More and more," Keller wrote, "I can see that the [Kennedy] children were catching the idea of Maryknoll."

Keller took a particular interest in young John F. Kennedy, who had just returned from study in England. He reported:

> Had a long talk with Jack Kennedy, who is putting out a book which the editor of *Time* and *Fortune* says one million Americans should read and one hundred thousand must read. The title of it is, *While England Slept*. He is a lad who has a great future, but, unfortunately, has never been to a Catholic school and shows a defect in Faith in many ways despite the fact that he is very faithful in going to Mass, etc. I thought it would be well to spend some time with him, not only in clearing up many little points concerning religion but also in giving him an understanding of our work, in behalf of which he can exert a fine influence during the years to come. . . . In the evening there was a very fine gathering of people, whom they had invited for the talk and movies.

A short time after Keller returned to his desk in New York, he received this note from Mrs. Joseph P. Kennedy:

> It was such a pleasure having you for a long weekend and your visit bore so much fruit. Jack is already planning to try out your arguments on a pal of his this week at Edgarton and I know he will try to improve and amplify his knowledge as time goes on. I am so delighted because I am sure he will reap great benefits for himself and for others. He owes this interest and enthusiasm to you and I am most appreciative of your efforts. . . . We all hope to see you soon again.

Jack Kennedy visited Keller in New York City a few weeks later, along with Charlotte McDonnell and Michael Grace. A few years later, a cover story in *The Field Afar* featured Lieutenant John F. Kennedy, who had just survived the sinking of his P.T. boat in the war in the Pacific. Keller remained in touch with the Kennedys and attended Jack Kennedy's wedding in 1953. He remained convinced all his life that the "Christopher idea" had influenced Jack Kennedy and his younger brother, Robert, to enter politics.

Keller let no opportunity slip to influence the influential. At a dinner party in Rye, New York, just before World War II spread to America, he once more brought the conversation around to religion. Spyros Skouras, the host, stood up before the group and declared that he planned to give up his business—he was a theater owner and movie producer—in a couple of years. Then, he said, he was going to work with Keller to bring about the reunion of the Greek Orthodox and Roman Catholic churches. "I have often joked with him about this," wrote Keller, "and he seems to have taken it seriously." Skouras was a good friend years later when Keller sought to penetrate Hollywood with Christopher ideas.

Keller's interest in the sons and daughters of the wealthy went far beyond any financial benefit that might come to Maryknoll. He told them their privilege was an obligation to exert leadership for the service of humanity. He found weddings to be a perfect setting for reaching the kind of people he wanted to talk to. One such wedding—some considered it the social event of the decade—was the marriage of Anne McDonnell to Henry Ford II. It was particularly noteworthy because it involved the conversion of Ford, whose father was antagonistic to Catholicism. As a close friend of the McDonnells and their relations, the Thomas E. Murrays, Keller was a guest. Although Fulton Sheen performed the marriage ceremony, it was Keller who helped Anne and Henry to open their wedding gifts. The reception at Southampton was a sumptuous affair. Keller commented: "The luxury of the whole thing made me think more than a little, especially when I thought of the contrast of the missions. But there wasn't much I could do about it, just at the moment, anyway." The couple's divorce many years later came as a blow to Keller.

At the time, however, all was rejoicing. How Keller viewed such occasions emerges from this entry in his work diary:

> Met hundreds of friends, old and new, and concentrated in a particular way on those from Detroit because they can't be seen so often. . . . This is one of the best examples of the value of an affair like this; people can be met and a real friendship formed in the most casual way and yet more can be effected in a few

moments than would be possible by months of planning. . . . I drove down to Easthampton with the Firestones and the Flanagans. All the way down they talked of what they ought to be doing for our work among the Chinese, which was interesting in that it showed they were thinking along the right lines.

In that year when FDR was running for a third term, Keller was involved in a small way in the campaign of the Republican challenger, Wendell Willkie. He made the acquaintance of John W. Hanes, who had just resigned from the U.S. Treasury to work for Willkie. Asked by Hanes to suggest anything that could help his candidate, Keller advised that the campaign be conducted with "good humor." He wrote:

We said we thought it would be well for Mr. Willkie to check up the writings of Will Rogers, single out his most unusual and effective quips, put them on file cards, index them and then use them constantly in his talks and writings. We stressed the point that the best way to answer bitterness is with kindness and mentioned that one reason for his [Willkie's] captivating the American people in such a remarkable way was his ability to disagree in a pleasant manner without ever becoming disagreeable. Mr. Hanes liked this idea better than anything else.

James Keller's horizons now had broadened far beyond Maryknoll. In a report he made on a party he attended in Southampton that same summer, he showed how he responded to repeated inquiries about religion:

It was all past my bedtime, but it seemed worthwhile to stay on the job because these people are going to be in positions of leadership and will do a great deal of good or harm just depending on their point of view. While only an occasional one will become Catholic, yet it is quite possible to dispose them towards the great fundamentals of religion in a little session like this. Things they would pick up on such an occasion might have an eventual effect on hundreds and even thousands of persons. So there is more than ordinary satisfaction in it. It was 1:30 when I finally turned in.

Keller's success in disposing members of the country's economic and political elite toward religion and a higher sense of duty was, to him, a logical extension of his missionary vocation. His efforts put him on a collision course with the views of his Maryknoll superiors.

· 8 ·

Second Life

"We can conquer the Japanese with guns, but unless we conquer them with ideas—the ideas of Jesus of Nazareth—we will have lost the war."

James Keller

Toward the end of his life, Keller was confronted by a member of the Christopher office staff who declared: "I'm depressed. I'm forty years old today."

"Good," the priest replied. "You have only five years to wait."

"For what?" she said in surprise.

"For your life to begin. I founded the Christophers when I was forty-five. That's when my life began."

The years leading up to Keller's forty-fifth birthday had the elements of an ending as much as a beginning. His workload diminished somewhat as help arrived in the form of two priests—Father Joseph English and Father Albert Nevins—who became his understudies. John Martin was transferred from the Midwest to supplement Keller's vocation efforts.

Keller had served as managing editor of *The Field Afar* long enough to modernize the magazine by reducing its unwieldy size to a smaller format and trying to make its editorial content more readable for the general public. He had recommended hiring qualified lay people as assistant editors and sending priests on for journalistic training, but neither of these recommendations was acted upon for some years. In 1944, Keller was relieved of most of his editorial duties. He estimated that about one idea in twenty got approval from his cautious superiors.

As he approached the height of his powers, Keller gained nationwide attention as the coauthor of a best-selling book, *Men of Maryknoll*. He found its ingredients in the tales of Maryknollers interned by the Japanese and sent home from the Orient. Taking notes on their stories of heroism and narrow scrapes with death, he compiled the stories of Joe Sweeney, Barney Meyer, John Romaniello, and Sandy Cairns, among others. All were friends from seminary days. Their joys and sufferings were his.

Keller knew that, as a writer, he couldn't do his "men of Maryknoll" the justice he felt they deserved. Two literary agents, Gertrude Algase and Helen Rich, introduced him to Meyer Berger, a feature writer on the *New York Times*. Charles Scribner agreed to publish the book. With Berger's magic at the typewriter and Keller's cooperation, the book made the best-seller list in the fall of 1943. "Mike Berger taught me all I know about writing," said the grateful priest, and indeed, Berger was a master of colorful detail. He and Keller became good friends.

Excerpts from *Men of Maryknoll* appeared in the *Reader's Digest*. In an ambitious recycling attempt, Keller tried to have the book turned into a radio series on CBS, a play for Mike Todd and a movie for Spyros Skouras at Twentieth Century–Fox. He came close to pulling off this multimedia scoop—even to the point of persuading Spencer Tracy to star in the play—but the projects foundered on Maryknoll's refusal to allow the scriptwriters to take liberties with the text.

Willing to try anything—at least once—Keller wrote a screenplay himself. It depicted—none too convincingly—a newspaperman who chucked it all up to become a missionary. Leo McCarey, director of *Going My Way*, liked it, but James E. Walsh didn't. That ended Keller's screenwriting career.

Keller was consulted by Archbishop McNicholas on ways to achieve a "more effective penetration of Catholic ideals into American life and public opinion." There was nothing subversive about this; Catholics believed their ideals were nearly identical to those of America's Founding Fathers. The prelate suggested that Keller put some of his ideas into a formula that would be of practical assistance to the average Catholic in spreading his or her faith. Priests like John A. Ryan and Francis J. Haas, along with the editors of *America* and *Commonweal*, had given much thought to the country's political and economic problems, but the results of such think-ing had never gotten out to the country's 21 million Catholics, to say nothing of the nation as a whole. Charles Coughlin had captured the public's imagination, but his message was essentially a negative one. In Keller, McNicholas saw a man who might command a mass following with the patriotic and religious principles he felt were needed. Despite some misgivings about his own abilities, Keller said he would try.

Keller was strengthened in his resolve to start a nationwide move-ment by the writings of an English journalist, Michael de la Be-doyere, who wrote:

> The force of Christianity as a world-ordering influence can only be restored in the end if millions of Catholics throughout the world are fully instructed in regard to Catholic teaching on the State and led by the example and instruction of their pastors to effect the immense revolution that would result from genuine fidelity to that teaching. Has not that been the missing link in the past: the failure of Catholics over the centuries, even when their personal religion has been devoted, to appreciate the truth that full Catholicity requires an equal understanding of what is involved in the Church's teaching about citizenship and public affairs, and an equal fidelity to this?[1]

In Keller's view, everyone had a "bit of the missionary" in his or her heart. Abstract formulas had to be translated into personal terms. Early in 1945, as World War II was drawing to a close, Keller wrote a long article in a clergy magazine, *The American Ec-clesiastical Review*. It was his response to McNicholas' prodding, Bedoyere's challenge, and his own disquiet. He titled it: "What about the Hundred Million?" By Keller's reckoning, 100 million Americans had no formal ties to religion. Such people, he said, "were becoming less and less conscious of the great Christian fun-damentals that make possible their present way of life." He called for specialized training for priests so that they could lead their people to take a greater interest in their nonchurchgoing neighbors. For the first time in print, he gave the name "Christophers" to those who brought Christ to people who didn't know him or who were hostile to Christianity. He listed the spheres of influence where, he felt, Christian principles were sorely needed: education, communications, community involvement, labor, and government.

"Even if Communism disappeared overnight," Keller said in conclusion, "the responsibility of the Christian would still be a great one. . . . If we launch out in great numbers, if we build and plan and venture with daring courage and faith that Christ expects of His followers, we may be the means of salvation to untold millions."

The article was a repetition of the old Americanist theme in modern garb. It must have reminded Keller of the words of the priest who spoke to him outside that candy store one Sunday night in San Francisco: "There may be thousands of people whose salvation depends on what you may do for them as a priest." Only now, the agents of salvation were not merely priests. Everyone could be a missioner.

The article created a sensation. The first three reprints totalled 37,000. Father, later Cardinal, Richard Cushing of Boston ordered 5,000. Archbishop Joseph Ritter (now in St. Louis) asked for 500. Bishop William Griffin of Trenton requested 200. Response to the article gave Keller the first thing a national movement needed—a mailing list.

Bishop James E. Walsh, Maryknoll's superior, called the article a "stirring appeal." Clearly pleased by the favorable comments he was getting, Walsh commented: "You must have expended much thought on it, as the thesis is presented with great clarity and much force. . . . I think it is helpful and salutary to see Maryknoll taking a bit of a lead—at least on the suggestive side—in mission spirit as applied to this country."

Keller had more in mind than "taking a bit of a lead." By September 1945, he had made up his mind to launch out. He told the bishop that so many requests had reached him for a follow-up to his original article that he had written a small book and would like approval to have it published privately, at his brothers' expense. Its title was *The Priest and the Hundred Million*. Bishop Walsh didn't think much of it. In a memo to his Council, he wrote:

On reading this I also think: (1) it is entirely naïve, with no grasp of what a spiritual problem really involves; (2) that no book on home mission work should emanate from Maryknoll;

(3) that it contains no practical plan. It has some virtue as a stimulating outline of a need.

A Council member, Father Thomas Kiernan, was even less enchanted:

> My impression of Father Keller's writing and thinking on problems of this nature is that they are superficial, immature and on the emotional side. His enormous zeal drives him to expression but I doubt if he has the intellectual capacity or experience required to be an apostle of this kind. I find him lacking in balance. I have often wondered if his years on promotion, during which he has been denied an outlet for the inherent zeal he possesses, have not created a frustration in his psychological make-up. Now, in middle life, is he unconsciously trying to satisfy such a frustration by attacking a well-known problem but one which he has magnified in his mind and perhaps misunderstood?

The book was never published, but Keller's mind was made up. *The Priest and the Hundred Million* was a trial run—it became the basis of Keller's 1948 best-seller, *You Can Change the World.*

It was time for Keller to make his intentions known. In October 1945, he wrote to Charles McCarthy from Cleveland to the effect that for at least five years he had been convinced that he should start the Christopher movement. His spiritual director, he said, had been urging him for a year to do so. Keller insisted that the movement was nothing more than a wider application of the "formula of success" that Maryknoll had already demonstrated. He admitted to McCarthy that a "home mission" effort would probably not sit well with his superiors. Consequently, he was ready to withdraw from Maryknoll to carry it on. Keller asked McCarthy not to give the letter to James E. Walsh until he gave him the word.

McCarthy's own word was distinctly negative. In a memo, he commented: "This problem is not easy to solve. We must get him work to absorb his energies. I think he should go to the missions. There is a great field for his zeal in Japan, if it is not too late to tackle the language." Halfway around the world was about the right distance McCarthy would prefer his erstwhile friend to be.

Keller asked to have the letter delivered to Walsh. Then he wrote directly to his superior:

> I decided to wait until August 15th, when I was twenty years ordained, to bring this matter to your attention. And still I delayed even further. I prayed that two signs would be given me. The first, that I had no defect in health, and secondly, that some priest would come from somewhere to carry on this little corner of work for Maryknoll that I am doing in New York. Both of these requests have been fulfilled.

Keller tried to assure his superior that he was doing God's will. He compared his decision to launch the Christophers to his resolve to enter Maryknoll over his parents' objections. Keller suggested that the simplest course would be to withdraw from the society, but he didn't want to embarrass Maryknoll. He insisted that he thought Christopher work was more important than anything he could do for Maryknoll. If Maryknoll could not adopt it, then perhaps it could go under the direction of a group of bishops. He told Walsh that McNicholas had recommended that the Christopher movement should begin on an experimental basis—and not be presented to the bishops of the country until it was a working reality, not just a theory.

Walsh's reply, concurred in by his Council, was blunt:

> Since you feel this strong urge for direct mission work, we think it justifiable to place your name on the list for a mission assignment next June. . . . Obviously, your boundless energies and apostolic zeal have not been adequately absorbed by promotional work. . . . We will try to select a mission for you where the language problem would not prove too difficult for one of your age.

The reply, though not unexpected, came as a blow to Keller. John Martin, who was present when Keller opened it, said that his face fell and he spent a long time trying to control his emotions. Something had just died—and a new life was struggling to be born.

Keller framed this reply:

> It would frankly be a big relief for me to be convinced that I ought to wipe my hands of the whole thing. I find myself in

the same state of nausea as I was when I was first trying to decide whether to go on for the priesthood. I didn't want to, really, and yet I felt I should. And so likewise in this case, I fear I would not have a clear conscience if I did not follow the conviction that I should make the move that strikes me as necessary to help get this movement under way as soon as possible.

Toward the end of November, Walsh visited Keller at the Maryknoll house in New York City. He reported to his Council:

> I found Father Keller in the same frame of mind in regard to his recent proposal. I explained to him what the procedure would be in case he decides to take the step. He replied that he would do nothing in a hurry and, for the present, would continue to keep the matter in reflection and prayer. We need to do nothing further now unless and until he renews his proposal.

The stalemate lasted through the Christmas season of 1945. Then everything changed. On January 4, 1946, Keller was notified that he had been elected a delegate to the Maryknoll General Chapter, to take place the following August. As a delegate, he could not be assigned overseas.[2] The situation was described by Kiernan, one of James E. Walsh's Council members:

> The Council said that either he [Keller] had to become just a Maryknoller or leave the Society and devote all of his time to the Christophers, if he could get a bishop. But he didn't. Jim was no fool. He just sat down without making a decision. He knew that a new Chapter was coming, and he knew that we were all going to be thrown out on our ear, and so he just bided his time.[3]

For the first six months of 1946, Keller watched and waited— and worked. His long period of uncertainty was coming to an end.

For all practical purposes, his first career was over—and a new life was about to begin.

.9.

A New Chapter

"The United States will have, for the next 20 or 30 years, the leadership of the world in its hands."

James Keller

As the Chapter of August 1946 approached, more than a few Maryknollers debated what Keller's loss could mean to the society. A measure of his contribution may be gauged from a letter written around this time by Considine to McNicholas:

> I feel certain that even Father Keller himself does not realize how much he has meant to Maryknoll's vital development and what through Maryknoll he is contributing to the Church. I believe Maryknoll is strong today because we have a strong public relations department and Father Keller is accountable for 80 percent of our public relations development. Last year, he brought us personally $300,000 in cash, while almost 50 of our 183 vocations came through the little office he operates in New York. More important than his returns are the philosophy and methods which penetrate our public relations men, all the product of his genius and requiring the constant operation of his mind to assure improvement.

Although now actively promoting the Christopher idea, Keller tried to keep his mind on the Chapter. As a delegate, he submitted a long list of suggestions designed to prepare the society for the challenges of the postwar period. A number of them, though not adopted at the time, eventually became part of Maryknoll's program in later years.[1]

On the Christopher front, Keller had a relatively free hand, as long as he showed discretion. He made a point of keeping the New York chancery office informed of his unofficial Christopher doings, receiving assurances of cooperation from Cardinal Spellman and other officials. He also completely rewrote his rejected manuscript and had it privately printed as *The Priest and a World Vision*. In its hundred pages, Keller argued that the Japanese and other non-Christians had a right to feel cheated because the Gospel had not been preached to them. He appealed to the 38,000 priests in the United States to do their best to change the introverted mentality of their people and become more missionary-minded. Various bishops ordered quantities of the book and had them distributed to their priests, and the Catholic Book Club made it a monthly selection.

A second magazine article, "You Can Be a Christopher," was printed in *The Catholic World*, a magazine published by the Paulist Fathers, in January 1946. In his typically patriotic fashion, Keller told the story of a recent celebration in the Los Angeles Memorial Coliseum where 100,000 spectators had witnessed a display of military strength. Suddenly the lights were turned off and the master of ceremonies told the multitude: "Perhaps you sometimes say to yourself, 'My job isn't important because it's such a little job.' But you are wrong. The most obscure person can be a very important person. Anyone here who wants to exert a far-reaching power may do so. Let me show you what I mean."

The emcee struck a match in the darkened arena, which was plainly seen by everybody. "Now," he said, "you can easily see the importance of one little light. . . . But suppose we all strike a light." As the stadium lit up with nearly 100,000 matches, Keller recounted that "everyone gasped in surprise. . . . Everyone present had received a lasting impression of the power of even one individual." It was a reenactment of Keller's experience years before when a single match had been lighted in the Metropolitan Opera House.

In "You Can Be a Christopher," Keller returned to the theme of the Hundred Million Americans who, he said, did not practice any religion. He quoted with approval an editorial in *Fortune*, which declared: "As the leading democracy of the world . . . the United States is perforce the leading practical exponent of Christianity. . . . The basic teachings of Christianity are in its blood stream.

The central doctrine of its political system—the inviolability of the individual—is a doctrine inherited from nineteen hundred years of Christian insistence upon the immortality of the soul. . . . The American has always been, and still is, at home among ideals. Now, manifestly, the American owes all this to the Church."

Keller called upon Christians to remind the Hundred Million of the "precious heritage of the Christian tradition." Arrayed against them, he said, were the "anti-Christian movements" which used "every possible medium—government, education, labor, press, movies, radio, comic strips, magazines, books and countless other channels—to further their purposes. . . . Their program is well organized, unusually efficient, remarkably aggressive." In other words, they were ten feet tall.

Keller gave the example of Nazi Germany, where "the 'good' people were taking care of themselves (while) the 'bad' people were taking care of the world." Keller reminded his readers of the early Christians who, despite persecution, "fired by the Holy Spirit . . . went forth as Christbearers, as Christophers. . . . Gradually they replaced brutality with love and gentleness; brought ideals of justice into government and business. Men and women who were addicted to the grossest forms of abuse and immorality began to recognize the sacred character and nobility of the human body, the sanctity of marriage and of the home."

Although he conceded that specially trained workers were essential for the more complex problems,[2] Keller asserted: "There are probably a million lay persons in our country today who are willing and anxious to play the role of Christophers in many walks of life."

Though considerably shorter than *What about the Hundred Million?*, "You Can Be a Christopher" reached a wider readership and produced an even more enthusiastic response. The conclusion of the article shows the sense of urgency that was a Keller hallmark:

> There is no time to lose. We must show speed. The efforts of even the least among us can be blessed with results that will exceed the fondest hopes of anyone. God is behind us. He will supply His grace in abundance. It may be the most unusual opportunity in history to recapture the world for Christ. It is a great time to live.

It was certainly a great time for James Keller to live. Although he was still uncertain about the attitude of Maryknoll's incoming leadership, his days of agony and nausea were over. While continuing to direct the activities of the Maryknoll house in New York, he kept his fences mended with local archdiocesan authorities. Encouraged by Spellman and other bishops, Keller sponsored May Day ceremonies to counter the traditional Communist demonstrations held on that day. Writing to bishops across the country, he suggested that they hold public gatherings in convenient outdoor places to pray for the conversion of Russia. It was a concrete action; it built on something Catholics were used to doing and, where the crowds were large, drew attention to the (one-man) organization that was behind it. By the early 1950s, when he began to deemphasize this aspect of his work, most of the dioceses in the United States and Canada were celebrating May 1 as Mary's Day, stealing some of the thunder from the Communists.

Keller now began to concentrate on the new administration elected by the Chapter to govern Maryknoll. Raymond A. Lane, a Maryknoll bishop from Manchuria, was chosen as the society's superior general in August 1946. Imprisoned by the Japanese and later repatriated, Lane shared Keller's opposition to Communism. Unlike his immediate predecessor, James Edward Walsh, Lane had a flair for publicity, an outgoing manner, and took a paternal interest in Keller and his new movement. Keller could not have asked for a more congenial superior—and he was to need one. Father Thomas S. Walsh, a China missioner who had also served briefly in one of Maryknoll's new missions in South America, became the group's vicar general, or second-in-command.

On August 13, 1946, when the new General Council of Maryknoll was settling in, Keller sent a five-page letter to Lane, in which he made three basic points: (1) the nation's 24 million Catholics would never take much interest in spreading the faith until they were aroused to show a personal concern in the people around them; (2) some priest from a mission group like Maryknoll was needed to stir up this interest; and (3) even a small movement, like the one he envisioned, could go a long way toward "saving America from Communism."

Keller asked Lane and his new Council to permit him to take a leave of absence to start this work, in the same manner that Maryknollers had been lent to dioceses to help out in the United States. He stated that he could easily continue to direct the Maryknoll operation in New York City,[3] but that he would be happy to step down if that was what his superiors wished.

Bishop Lane showed enthusiasm for the Christopher movement, and immediately requested several hundred copies of a Christopher pamphlet to distribute at a talk he was giving. Keller had found a sympathetic ear. With a freedom to express his opinions he had not enjoyed in ten years, Keller sent Lane this critique of *The Field Afar*:

> I am still convinced that we are putting out a job that does not click with the majority of our readers. We produce something that is much more according to our own mentality and taste rather than that of the person who sits in the pews of our average church and is the typical subscriber. With few exceptions, he is tossing a dollar our way to help a cause. The magazine is an appendage that he is not much interested in. He may glance at it the first time it comes to him but, in most cases, it does not catch, much less hold, his continued interest.

Keller estimated that this was true for about 70 percent of the magazine's readers. The rest, he said, were already "sold." He suggested hiring a firm to do a reader survey to find out whether he was right or wrong. Lane replied almost immediately, asking Keller to come up to Maryknoll as soon as possible to discuss the matter with Considine and McCarthy. Far from being ignored, Keller was being courted.

The Christophers did not remain a one-man show for long. Florence Okazaki, a pre-med student Keller had met at the Maryknoll house in Los Angeles the year before, joined him as office manager and general factotum, and remained with him for nearly 15 years. The Christopher staff soon included four assistants. The "couple of extra rooms" they used at the rear of Maryknoll's 39th Street house, threatened at times to crowd out the promotion office workers. But, since Keller was in charge of both, he was usually able to keep the peace.

To stay in regular touch with his growing list of interested people, Keller began sending them bimonthly bulletins called Christopher News Notes. As he spoke to audiences across the country, passing out cards wherever he went, the numbers receiving this free publication grew from 4,000 to about 40,000 in the first year and 800,000 by 1954. In the Notes he reported on his own activities or on the initiatives taken by people who caught the Christopher message—"one candle lights another."

One issue (#8, 1947) concerned a series of articles in the *Ladies' Home Journal* called "Letters to Joan." Keller felt that some of the pieces contained errors regarding the Christian concept of womanhood. He asked Charlotte McDonnell Harris, a young mother, to write a reply. Although she had never written before for publication, Harris put together a piece called "A Letter to Joan from a Catholic," which was printed in the magazine, reaching an audience of 4.5 million. Keller commented: "As a result, the changeless truth adapted to our changing times will reach millions who might otherwise never have had it brought to their attention, had not Mrs. Harris made the effort. That's reaching the multitude as Christ said we ought!"

Simply written and loosely organized, Christopher News Notes contained information on current events of significance to the movement, accounts of what other "Christophers" were doing, and exhortations to "go and keep going." They were Keller's main link with his growing audience. The movement had no actual memberships, meetings, or dues. Each person was left free to put Christopher principles into practice as he or she saw fit. The dominant note that ran through these leaflets was that of hope mixed with a sense of urgency in the face of possible disaster. But the hopefulness predominated.

In the category of current events, the peril of Communism was uppermost. Communism was a religion, Keller told his readers (#4, 1946), quoting Jacques Duclos, secretary of the French Communist party. Its adherents in the United States, he said, "swarmed" into the mass media because they knew that the writer, especially the scriptwriter, "determines the message that reaches the millions of radio listeners and moviegoers." Communists worked to control writers' associations, he insisted, hoping to "throttle the literary work of non-Communists." Keller urged unremitting prayer for the conversion of Russia and special prayers for Stalin and Mao Tsetung. "Our very survival as a free nation," he wrote (#53, 1953), "depends on our facing up to grim realities. This cannot be brought about by legislation alone or coercion." Instead, he declared that Communism could be overcome by millions of individuals showing a "sense of urgency," and by stirring up public opinion against the Reds' "honeyed promises." Keller accepted the prevailing view (#53) of a Communist conspiracy that had "started twenty years ago and is still going (that) has helped to shape our domestic and foreign policies." This conspiracy, he believed, helped bring about the "loss of China" to the Communists.

Keller's anti-Communism was never strident, nor did he advocate McCarthyite witch hunts. In fact, Senator McCarthy, who dominated the news during the early 1950s, never got so much as a mention—pro or con—in the Christopher News Notes. In keeping with his "positive approach," Keller told his readers to show the same vision and daring that the Communists did—to beat them at their own game. Keller was close to the Catholic conservative voices (*The Brooklyn Tablet* and *Our Sunday Visitor*) in his detestation of Communism, but not far from the liberals (*America* and *Commonweal*) in his insistence on constitutional guarantees. To the consternation of both sides in the internal security debate, Keller sidestepped specific issues and condemnations.

Americanism was another theme in the early Christopher News Notes (1946–1955). Keller quoted with approval the words of Bing Crosby: "It is the American way to believe in God. There can be no real brotherhood of man without the Fatherhood of God." Keller's sense of America's global role was less a matter of "manifest destiny" than a point of fact. "For the present, at least," he wrote (#12, 1949), "as America goes, so goes the world." He left it open as to who might lead the world in the future. Keller's use of patriotism was religious in intent. He praised the woman in Stamford, Connecticut, who fought against heavy odds to have the motto "In God We Trust" prominently displayed in her local junior high school. He wrote (#43, 1952): "She decided that if we Americans put 'In God We Trust' on our coins, the least we can do is put it in our schools." Keller advocated that historical facts of a moral and spiritual nature be taught in every school in the land, such as references to God in the Declaration of Independence and other early documents, the invocations of the Deity by many of the nation's Founding Fathers and in every Presidential inaugural address—in effect, the evidence for a consensus on Judeo-Christian values at the nation's founding. This theme he developed more fully in his 1953 book, *All God's Children*.

Accounts of what other Christophers were doing abounded in these early News Notes. Keller made bold to say (#42, 1952): "As a result of Christopher talks, News Notes, books and movies, we estimate that 100,000 persons have gone into the fields that count or have taken on a new sense of purpose if already there." These "dedicated apostles" came from all walks of life—from movie producers, ex-servicemen, and housewives, to taxi drivers and atomic scientists. A barber in Southampton, New York (#43, 1952), started a letter-writing campaign to have Americans urge their relatives in Italy to "think twice about the way they voted in the critical Italian election . . . in April, 1948. . . . The campaign eventually reached a total of ten million letters. Even the Communists themselves admit that it was this flood of letters that turned the tide against them." Keller felt that defeating the Communist threat meant not military superiority alone but superiority in ideas.

The News Notes gave multiple examples of men and women who left well-paying jobs to take lower salaries as teachers. Keller urged taxpayers to support teachers' demands for more adequate salaries, to cooperate with them—and to know what their children were being taught. He emphasized the need for more and better-trained social workers, pointing out that social service was one of the best ways of carrying out the words of Christ: "feed the hungry . . . harbor the homeless . . . visit the sick." Keller called attention to an atomic scientist (#54, 1953) in Schenectady, New York, who, together with several others, entered the field "because of Christopher emphasis on the power for good in the atomic energy field." These scientists, he told his readers, made their career decision because they saw the atom as a "gift of God and (to be) used for research in medicine, industry and agriculture, as well as for defense." In the same issue of News Notes, Keller told the story of a woman who had served six years in the Georgia legislature. "She is doing everything she can to encourage competent people to enter politics," he commented, "as well as to spark those already in the field with a renewed sense of purpose."

Keller deplored the sale of warlike Christmas toys, including one advertisement for a "lifesize atom bomb set and toy poison gas." He added: "We may be getting a little too close to a means employed by totalitarians who used even toys to dispose children towards brutality." He approved of the trend to "put Christ back into Christmas" through religious greeting cards and public observances stressing the religious character of the day.

Disturbed as he was about books that promoted "subversion, atheism and immorality," Keller urged his followers to "be fair about it" (#40, 1951). "To counteract this dangerous practice," he said, "a few upright citizens advocate the opposite policy of pushing good books and holding back those they regard as evil. That is an oversimplified answer to a complicated problem. Great care should be taken to avoid the very abuse these worthy citizens rightly condemn." He advised such indignant persons not to take the law into their own hands but "to proceed with the utmost honesty, respect for the rights of others and through the recognized channels of legitimate authority." Keller was no book-burner.

In a special publication (1947), "Calling Christopher Writers!," Keller announced a writing contest, with $30,000 in prize money. He said, ". . . we feel a particular responsibility to awaken Catholics to the dynamic contributions they can make. . . . But do most Catholics share with others this spiritual and cultural heritage as they should? Unfortunately not. . . . Between 20 and 25 of every 100 Americans are Catholic. Yet the proportion of Catholic writers is very small. . . . How often we (Catholics) use a terminology and point of view that puzzles or even repels non-Catholics." Keller felt that "writing can be a labor of love, a living prayer, a work that will ennoble and sanctify both you and all who read what you have written."

Writing was the backbone and, in some ways, the bane of Keller's existence. He never found it easy, and it was even harder to find—and keep—anyone who could express his ideas in a way that suited him.

In all his writings, talks, and broadcasts, Keller saw himself as a missionary (#12, 1948): "We are merely applying to the heart of America the same simple approach used by a Maryknoller in bringing Christ into a pagan city in China. Instead of sitting on the outskirts of the city, complaining or criticizing, he goes in—as Christ said to do—and puts into literal effect an old Chinese proverb: 'It is better to light one candle than to curse the darkness.' Even if only one missioner goes into the city, it is better one than none at all. Even if he makes no apparent progress, or is persecuted and imprisoned, nevertheless he is *there!*"

All was not rosy on the Maryknoll front. James E. Walsh, the retired Superior General, stuck to his original opinion about the Christopher movement. It was nearly two years old when Walsh wrote to the Maryknoll Council: "He [Keller] ought to sell his plan to some American bishop, or let it alone." Nor did Keller avoid some cautionary comments from Thomas S. Walsh, who looked over Christopher materials before they were printed. The vicar general counseled Keller not to play down religious differences when appealing to Protestants. "Though we invite the cooperation of Protestants in combating Communism," he wrote, "we don't want to give them the impression that we have abandoned our distinctive position. . . . I am afraid that this whole passage will leave you open to such criticism on the part of precise-minded Catholics."

Neither Maryknoll nor Keller was very "precise-minded" when it came to figuring out his role as head of the Maryknoll house and his position as head of the Christophers. In the first few years of the movement, Keller moved around the country, covering in one swing twenty cities in as many days. Inevitably his Maryknoll work began to slide. It bothered the exacting Charles McCarthy, who sent this memo to the Council in March 1948:

> [In January] I had the assurance of Father Keller that the Christophers were well established and were rolling full steam on their own and that, consequently, he would be able to devote most of his time to Maryknoll work. I must have misunderstood Father Keller because, a few days after I made my proposal to the Council, I received a letter from him saying he was going away on a lecture tour. I don't think he has been in New York City for one full week since sometime in January. The New York City house has suffered for a year-and-a-half from lack of proper direction.

And, true enough, Keller did get around. In November 1947, for example, he made this report to Bishop Lane on his breakneck pace:

Have been on the hop quite a bit since a week ago when I gave
four talks at the University of West Virginia; two the next day
in St. Louis; three others in Michigan (Adrian, Bloomfield and
Birmingham); three in Cincinnati, and then on to Bean Town
for three more there after a brief stopover. Three more tonight
and tomorrow in Washington, and winding up the rest of the
week with talks each night in New York, New Brunswick,
Brooklyn and Philadelphia.

Shortly after McCarthy's memo, he and Considine met with
Keller to review the personnel situation. Out of it emerged a de-
cision to groom Father Joseph English to be Keller's understudy
and eventual replacement. Fathers James Courneen and Walter
Maxcy were to be the "road men." Maxcy gave this assessment of
Keller's role in the development of Maryknoll:

> Maryknoll was blessed in its growing days with the triumvirate
> of three men who, I believe, didn't really hit it off as friends,
> but were dedicated to Maryknoll and its ideals. Considine was
> the dreamer and schemer. Charlie McCarthy could manufacture
> and package the plans. And J. K. was the salesman. The dis-
> tinction shouldn't be pushed too far, for J. K. was the man who
> came up with the sponsor idea.[4]

Maxcy recalled that, on one occasion, he received a directive
from McCarthy to send out vocational notes by metered mail instead
of stamps. Maxcy said: "J.K. hit the ceiling. 'We're losing the
personal touch,' he said. 'Don't let Charlie get away with this!' But
it ended up with: 'Charlie is the boss, so you have to do what he
says—but never stop fighting him on it.' "
Maxcy alluded to Keller's penchant for making lemons into lem-
onade. In the late 1940s, all of Maryknoll was in an uproar because
the Archdiocese of New York decided to limit the society to five
church dates a year, instead of the customary forty. Keller told his
assistants: "Pick up those dates tomorrow, January 2, and then you
have 363 days left for promotional work." Maxcy found this "sort
of typical of him to see an apparent setback as a chance to step
forward."
Motivation for promotion work was another area in which Keller

differed from his coworkers, and even from his earlier practice. According to Maxcy:

> If he were to do it again, Keller said, instead of selling Mary-knoll, he would have developed the idea of *everyone* being a missionary, the idea of the Christophers, and would have worked it into the foreign missions. . . . He balked at the campaign of selling Glen Ellyn [a seminary] to the people. Selling a building, instead of an idea. Where would the Jesuits be, Keller asked, if they were pushing the idea of Woodstock [another seminary] instead of the Company of Jesus?

For all of Keller's emphasis on the "personal touch," his preoccupation with time set definite limits on its practice. "The fellows from the Bowery who came to the door for a handout didn't see Jim very often," remembered Maxcy. "He'd get one of the other padres to take that one over." Keller was doing the work of two men—and perhaps more—at the time.

Father Jack King, who lived with Keller in the late 1950s, commented:

> Jim never seemed to "live" with others in the house. He took meals with us, and that was just about it. He was not much to mix with the others, to just talk and have a highball. He seemed to be in his own world. Of course, he was totally immersed in the Christophers at this time. So it would only be natural to "shut us out" of his life. . . . He would cannibalize the morning papers during breakfast. He carried with him a paper clipper and, when he saw an article that interested him, he immediately clipped it out. Anyone coming in late for breakfast never read a complete issue.[5]

Nor did Keller change much in the 1960s. As Father Joseph O'Neill recalled the man:

> In many ways, Jim Keller was somewhat of a loner. I don't think he had many close friends. He certainly was one of our best-known Maryknollers, but I never saw him with many close friends. He had a limited time for sociabilities. Yet, he was full of stories, humorous anecdotes.[6]

Maryknoller Dennis Powell remembered Keller losing his temper once.[7] It concerned Monsignor John Romaniello, a flamboyant Maryknoll missioner from China. "He told Jim Keller," Powell related, "that his Christopher work was nothing but 'do-goodism.' Jim got upset and excused himself from the table. That was the first and only time I ever saw him flustered and angry."

To Father Frank McKay, three years spent with Keller were the loneliest in his life. He said:

> Keller was an enigma. He could write about human feelings, charity and communication. But he couldn't do it himself. I spent three years with him and never knew him. If I had a choice of someone with whom to spend three years on a desert island, I would never pick Jim Keller.[8]

McKay, a Californian, maintained contact with Keller's family in Oakland who, he said, were always waiting, usually in vain, for Keller to visit them. Then he added:

> He considered himself almost without father and mother. His brother Lou, the plumber, was very unlike Jim. Lou supervised the digging of a four-foot trench for a water pipe at the Mountain View Seminary. Lou would swear like a trooper and refer to his "stodgy, stiff brother."

Keller walked a thin line between Maryknoll and the New York Archdiocese. In 1948, he criticized the draft of a statement about to be issued by the society to clarify its relationship with the Christophers. He wrote:

> The suggested item on responsibility conveys nothing about a bishop keeping an eye on the project, which Archbishop McNicholas said was the chief precaution the hierarchy would wish. Bishop Lane could and should do this as a member of the hierarchy. . . .
> If this is omitted, Cardinal Spellman would justly conclude that this project is hanging in mid-air and might take the whole thing over two days later.

Keller had a point. Once Maryknoll gave him permission to start the Christophers and allowed him to use the New York house as its base of operations, it is hard to see how it could deny responsibility for, and even endorsement of, the organization. The Maryknoll Council tried in 1949 and 1950 to shift responsibility to the archdiocese, but Cardinal Spellman never acted.

While all this activity was going on behind the scenes, Keller was preparing to launch a book that would always be identified with the Christopher movement.

·10·

You Can Change the World

"The big need, therefore, is to encourage people with good ideas to go into the marketplace rather than to concentrate too much on driving out those with evil designs."

James Keller

If James Keller was open to the charge of vagueness when he started the Christopher movement, *You Can Change the World* did much to dispel that impression. Written in snatches and spurts during the hectic days of 1947 and through the summer of 1948, the book was a detailed handbook of what Keller was asking of the American people—and, indeed, all people of good will.

Much of the preliminary work on the book was done by Charles Oxton, a newspaperman and novelist. Drawn largely from previous Christopher News Notes and Keller's extensive files, the book bears the author's unmistakable imprint. Keller's previous books appealed mostly to the clergy or his fellow Catholics. This volume reached out to all who were seeking positive solutions to the problems of humanity.

Keller submitted the manuscript to his friend, Fulton Oursler, senior editor of the *Reader's Digest*.[1] Oursler looked over the untitled draft and his eye caught the phrase, "you can change the world." He told Keller that this should be the title, and predicted that it would be a best-seller. He was right. Keller also showed the draft to Father Frederick McManus of the National Catholic Welfare Conference and to two Jesuits, one of them an expert on the papal encyclicals. They assured him of its doctrinal orthodoxy.

On the Maryknoll side, both Considine and Father John

McConnell, a Scripture expert, went over the text. And McConnell, for one, did give it the eagle eye. McConnell said of this volume and other Christopher books which he scrutinized for Keller:

> I used to slash his English and his use of Scripture, just tear it to pieces. I don't think he batted an eye. . . . I thought his English was awful, and all I could think of was Mrs. Roosevelt. She was, of course, very powerful with many people for the same reason. She never flinched from repeating the same dull truism. Neither did Jim. I mean, he could say it a thousand times, three thousand times, just as sincerely and effectively as he could the first. . . . He had really no grasp as far as I could see of any kind of scholarly point of view. You had always to be rescuing him from monstrous fundamentalistic statements. If he had gone on to study, he may have been different.[2]

McConnell's "slashing" had its effect. The book was well-written, though some might question its presuppositions. Keller himself had no illusions about it, as emerges from this letter which accompanied a copy of the manuscript sent to Bishop Lane:

> We have been purposely repetitious. The book is not intended to be read in one sitting—as a novel— but used as a reference or guidebook, with sections of it adapted to specific groups. We are afraid some would miss the purpose, for instance, if they single out a chapter on writing, or "Influencing the World from the Home," and did not find in it sufficient emphasis on the spirit and purpose behind the Christophers.

If James Keller was modest about *You Can Change the World*, he was also proud of it. In the same letter to Lane, he said:

> We don't expect our book will be any world-beater. We are conscious of many imperfections in it. One thing in its favor, however—as far as we can check—there isn't anything else like it on the market, or we would have copied part of it! We have had to start off from scratch.

You Can Change the World, in its nineteen chapters, is both a tribute to the power of Communism and an appeal to believers in God to become as active as the Communists in promoting their own beliefs. The first sentence in the introduction contains one of those easy-to-remember formulas that Abbé de la Maitre had said the Nazis used to such effect: "Did you ever stop to think that the United States is being effectively undermined by less than one percent of the people in our country, of whom only a portion are Communists?" He called on one percent of the population to compete with the Communists and replace them in the fields of influence. Where did he get this figure? Possibly, he made it up, as it served to illustrate a point.

He used the story in St. John's Gospel of the Samaritan woman who carried the message of Jesus to her townspeople, as an example that God could use anybody of good will to do his work. Married five times and a heretic to boot, she *was* an unlikely messenger.

Keller found a precedent for his gradualist approach in Pope Gregory, who in the sixth century sent Augustine to England to convert the Britons—not to destroy their temples but to transform them into churches and to change their practices into Christian festivals. Even if people had but "one percent of the truth," he felt, encouragement might lead them to its fullness.

You Can Change the World did not treat thoroughly the field of government service. This he reserved for a later book. He did talk about Communist infiltration in labor unions, which was a hotly contested topic in the late 1940s.[3] Repeatedly, he insisted on beating the Communists at their own game by running for office, learning parliamentary procedure, and staying at meetings till the bitter end.

In his chapter on writing, the various means of popular communication were treated in detail. Even the infant medium of television received notice, for its potential in 1948 was just beginning to be understood.

Keller had a firm belief in the value system of the average person. "Do not worry about your sense of judgment," he said. "The average American mother and father are well blessed with common sense, fairness and safe norms of decency." His book made no scholastic distinctions about who was or was not qualified to take a stand on matters of public policy.

In the chapter on business, Keller devoted three pages of tribute to his friend, Basil Harris of U.S. Lines, who had just died. Harris was respected by management and labor alike as a "man of his word." One associate of his was quoted as saying: "I don't know of anyone who has gone to him in search of a job that he hasn't helped. I take off my hat to him. Most of us give money, but Basil does that and more. He gives his time. He gives himself!"

What troubled Keller about business people was not their desire to make a profit but the tendency to accumulate wealth for its own sake, or for the sake of power, while neglecting other, more important dimensions of life. He said:

> Often a businessman will give a new wing to a college or university, yet have little or no idea of what will be taught in the building he donated. Not infrequently, the very principles for which he stands will be undermined in the classrooms he built.

Keller enjoined "Christopher-minded employers" to "treat workmen as *free* people, as copartners in ownership, profits, and management, and thus avoid extremes of both left and right." He quoted in some detail from the two major papal encyclicals on labor, *Rerum Novarum* (1891) and *Quadragesimo Anno* (1931). Because of its relative strength, Keller declared that management had an even greater obligation toward social justice than did labor. Along with most Catholic thinkers, he saw government's role in labor-management as a limited one. He cited with approval the words of Father Raymond A. McGowan, director of the Social Action Department of the National Catholic Welfare Conference:

> American labor does not look forward to being superseded some time by an all-owning, all-employing, all-trading, all-governing government. American labor has thought of its own personal dignity and personal responsibilities. So I place the American labor movement along with religion in the first line of defense against a totalitarian America.

To students, Keller emphasized the need to activate their beliefs in the classroom and in student movements—doing all out of a spirit of love. He urged them to avoid the attitude of the Gestapo: "Is my neighbor a Communist?" Rather, he recommended the spirit of the parable (Luke 10—the Good Samaritan), "Is a Communist my neighbor?"

To those who stressed personal sanctification Keller said:

It is so easy, strangely enough, for those who devote themselves most faithfully to spiritual exercises to become over-solicitous about saving self, body and soul, while ignoring the pitiful plight of the vast numbers over the earth who are starving—physically, mentally and spiritually.

Perhaps the clearest statement of the Christopher purpose comes through in this passage:

It is much more than the dollars, food, medicine and material things of America that the world needs and really wants. What they crave, above all else, is the spirit that makes America the great nation it is. And that spirit, above all else, is God's truth proclaiming through the Declaration of Independence, the Constitution,[4] and the Bill of Rights that even the least individual as a child of God has rights that no man or nation can take from him—the right to life, to liberty, and to the pursuit of happiness which begins here, but which will have its supreme fulfillment in eternity.

The paperback edition of *You Can Change the World*, which was 364 pages long, was reprinted many times through the 1960s. At least 300,000 copies were distributed. Through this book, Keller popularized Catholic—especially papal—social teaching perhaps more than anyone before him.

Reviews of the book were generally favorable. *The Saturday Review* gave it more pluses than minuses: "It is naïve, insouciant, repetitious, and all the other things readers are apt to call writing which is disorganized and amateurish. But it has something which can make it an epic—a simple, explosive, contagious idea. And, if ideas are as important as we have been taught to believe, this one may in truth 'change the world.' "

"Many sincere Christians," said the *New York Times*, "will find themselves unable to follow Father Keller in all the specific judgments he sets down. This is not to deny the wisdom and stimulation to be found in these pages. Anyone who follows the regimen outlined here will, in a number of ways, help himself and his society. He will also be a very busy man."

The *Library Journal* wrote of the book as "a positive answer to the Communists and the Godless rather than the negative, with which we have been too long familiar," and recommended it highly for all libraries.

Syndicated columnists George Sokolsky and Bob Considine were lavish in their praise. Considine spoke more of the movement itself: "In its comparatively short campaign, the Christopher movement has made itself felt in certain labor unions, Hollywood, industrial plants, offices, education, social service, writing and a host of other fields."

The *American News,* in its recommendations to book dealers and newsstands, stated: "This book is not the work of fanatical bias. It is wise, as well as eloquent, and it would not be surprising to see it take hold for one of those quietly increasing circulations by the word-of-mouth route."

Not everybody got on the bandwagon. *Integrity,* a Catholic magazine that stressed spiritual formation, the works of mercy, and flight from the commercial world, found it full of "modern clichés" and "pious slogans." The reviewer, Carol Jackson, minced no words:

> This book seems to cling to the natural level of goodness and to place undue hope of real accomplishment therein. Occasionally the supernatural life is mentioned, but not very often. And there is no real stress put on frequenting the sacraments. The Declaration of Independence seems almost interchangeable with the Ten Commandments, and the defense of American democracy nearly synonymous with the defense of the Church.

Jackson seemed particularly offended because there was no explicit mention of such groups as Catholic Action, the Legion of Mary, Friendship House, and the Catholic Worker. Keller sent the review to Bishop Lane with this comment:

> *Integrity* is on the sour side too, because things are coming so easy for us, and because we say that "little people" can do big things. Their criticism is a scorcher. It will do us a lot of good.

In a subsequent issue of News Notes, Keller printed many favorable reviews of *You Can Change the World,* and undertook to rebut—though not by name—the *Integrity* criticisms. Agreement was not likely, however. *Integrity* believed that spiritual formation was a precondition to effective action, while the Christophers stressed action as a means of spiritual formation.

Another critical review of *You Can Change the World* came from the pen of Edward S. Skillin, editor of *Commonweal* (12/17/48). After praising the book's purpose, he said:

> In the Christopher analysis—here questions begin to pop up in my mind—it is in the various media communicating ideas that a million wicked people are engaged in foisting their Marxism, anti-religionism, attacks on Christian marriage and the natural law, etc., on the unsuspecting American people. I have always been skeptical about the villain thesis of history and I wonder how aptly it can apply here.

In Skillin's thesis, American materialism—and not Marxism—was the real obstacle to the advance of Christianity. Then he asked how much of an impact one person could have at a place like *Time* magazine:

> Can a lone Christopher, or even several Christophers—equipped as they are—actually make any real impact on such a pachyderm? My guess is that, as Christophers, their presence there would be virtually meaningless.

Skillin, like *Integrity*, raised the question of spiritual formation, but expressed pleasure at the news that Christians were entering the fields of education, government, labor, and the media—a happy contrast, to his mind, to the usual Catholic posture of "red-baiting."

Keller wrote a long letter of response. In it he tried to dispel Skillin's notion that the Christophers' main emphasis was on the "communications arts" or that most of the damage was being done by Communists. As to the contention that a few Christophers working at *Time* would be meaningless, Keller replied:

> This guess, of course, might be correct if those going as Christophers had no faith, no hope, no charity, but this guess would not necessarily apply to a follower of Christ. . . . In short, we have a humble, and sincere, confidence in the power of God's grace to work His Will among men through the instruments of His Creation.

As to spiritual formation, Keller responded:

> There are nearly 200,000 priests, brothers and sisters now engaged in the important task of emphasizing the necessity of personal formation. It was with *specific intent*, therefore, that we did not dwell on this element but confined our Christopher appeal to one small facet of a big problem: *purpose* and a *sense of direction* for everyone, but especially for little people.

Although the Maryknoll Council approved Keller's letter for publication, he never sent it. Thirty-three years later, Edward Skillin, now publisher of *Commonweal*, was shown Keller's letter. He responded:

> Thanks for the chance to read Father Keller's reaction to my review. Aside from the point about the number of Marxists, etc., he is probably right that one should rely more on the grace of God, as one encounters our world, than I indicated. Related to that is the question of 'formation' which I felt was so neglected in the book. *Formation*, as I thought of it then—and still do— was *not* so much in terms of training and *information* as of *metanoia* [conversion]—which would be something more than a willingness to go out and confront the wicked world. Formation such as this is not a matter of a day.
>
> Too bad Father Keller never wrote us that article. I greatly enjoyed re-reading my review (how little things have changed, except for the nuclear arms race), and Fr. Keller's temperate rejoinder was good to consider.[5]

Whatever the merits of individual parts of the book, *You Can Change the World* gave hope to thousands of people who might otherwise have decided to do nothing in the public interest. It stirred the dormant energy and latent idealism of people who may have had a Christian upbringing but who needed a "salesman" like Keller to stir them to action.

It was precisely a *metanoia*, or change of heart, that *You Can Change the World* wrought in the lives of many readers. Typical of the thousands of letters generated by the book was one written in 1952 by a mother in Long Island, New York:

I am half finished reading *You Can Change the World* and you have changed my way of thinking. The realization that any little constructive thing we do is a part of a large movement for the better is an inspiring thought. I am the mother of a four-year-old child, a housewife living in the suburbs and you have given a new purpose to my everyday activities. Although I have received a Catholic education, you are the first person who has filled me with the desire to LIVE my religion.

Thinking along Christopher lines for only a few weeks, my first efforts have been feeble ones but I am not discouraged. . . . (1) I have joined a discussion group whose leader is a sincere Christopher. (2) I have made a point of visiting or writing to every sick friend I have and try to leave with them a constructive idea or do them some little kindness. (3) I arranged for two friends, one a teacher, the other a school principal, to receive your "News Notes."

Another woman, in Los Angeles, wrote that she had "rattled around in a big house, bored silly" until she caught the Christopher message. "The idea that impressed me most about it," she wrote, "was living as a Christopher without wearing a big sign on my forehead that said, 'I am a Christopher.' I never talk about it, never mention it, except that once or twice someone has said, 'You act like a Christopher,' and I smile."

She said that, after reading *You Can Change the World* and another Christopher book, "they made me itch." Her first action was to answer a call to jury duty, which led her—despite the lack of a college degree—to study law. She passed an equivalence and law aptitude test, enrolled in law school and was maintaining a B+ average. She continued:

Always in the back of my mind is the knowledge that I am a Christopher. I don't do anything worldshaking, but I have my own methods, best suited to my own temperament. God endowed me with certain talents, and I don't believe He would have given them to me if He didn't want me to use them. I have an understanding heart, for instance, that can often see into the causes of behavior. . . . I spent most of my own life as an intimidated individual—*until* I got it straight in my mind that I owed humility *only* to God, and that letting anyone else intimidate me was bowing down before a false idol.

Her letter concluded:

> Anyway, as you have guessed, I am no longer bored, nor dis-
> contented. I no longer feel out of the . . . mainstream of life. I
> feel that I live each day fully, facing and accepting the challenges
> and opportunities that I meet, I am fulfilling the purpose for
> which I was brought into this world, and am growing towards
> the challenges and opportunities that may come in the fu-
> ture. . . . What if I had never become a *secret* Christopher?

But there was probably one letter above all that gave a feeling
of satisfaction to James Keller as the result of *You Can Change the
World*. It came from a one-time critic and adversary, who had been
turned by the volume into a friend and supporter. Dated November
29, 1949, the letter bore a Shanghai postmark. It read:

> Dear Jim:
>
> I liked your book immensely—*You Can Change the World*—and
> a friend of mine here, a very wealthy banker of Jewish race, is
> reading it now, and seems to like it equally. He wants to pass
> around the book among some friends, so I told him by all means
> to do so. What we both liked in it particularly was the spirit of
> charity that breathes in it, the consideration shown for all points
> of view, the care used to avoid offending sensibilities while
> stating the Catholic attitude with every frankness.
>
> I must say I was amazed at the very effective streamlined
> style of the presentation—a sufficiently difficult feat, I should
> think, in view of the repetitious nature required by the theme.
> Short sentences, plenty of apt illustrations, and a sparing jour-
> nalistic style evidently made a good recipe to solve such a prob-
> lem. . . .
>
> As for Shanghai, I simply love the place and the people. It's
> a wonderful town—that anybody can turn upside down but
> nobody can ever daunt or discourage; and in my old age I find
> it is developing my long neglected sense of humor. Happy
> Christmas, if this reaches you at that time, or even if it doesn't.
>
> Devotedly in Xt.,
> J. E. Walsh, M. M.

• *11* •

Learning from the Communists

*"Strive to be motivated by a consuming desire to bring the
love and truth of Christ to all mankind to right the wrongs
that the Communists exploit—and no study, work or sacrifice will be too great for you."*

James Keller

Whittaker Chambers was a name that made headlines in the late
1940s. He attended Columbia University, where his disillusion-
ment with the Western democracies led him to join the Communist
party in 1925 and later to act as a courier in an espionage ring.

Chambers broke with Communism before World War II and
went to work for *Time* magazine. He revealed his clandestine activities to the security division of the State Department, but nothing
came of his charges for nine years. Among his assertions was that
Alger Hiss, a former State Department official, had been his chief
contact in the underground.

In 1948, both Chambers and Hiss testified before the House
Committee on Un-American Activities. Chambers told all he knew,
while Hiss denied he had ever been a Communist. At first, public
opinion favored the respectable, Harvard-educated Hiss and dis-
counted the witness of Chambers.

Eventually, a Grand Jury in New York indicted Hiss for perjury.
It was during the sensational trial of Hiss that Chambers, in despair
of ever clearing his name, made an appointment to see Keller.
The two men had never previously met, though it is probable that
Chambers knew of Keller's anti-Communism. As the troubled man

entered Keller's office in the spring of 1949 and asked for guidance, the priest reached into a pile of daily meditations on which he had been working. The selection he chose began with these words: "Good Friday is a day of failure, but failure only from a human point of view." The passage concluded: "With each of us, the failure of the cross must go before the final triumph. We must be willing to fail and fail again—even to be crucified—in order to play our part in saving the world." Chambers quickly scanned the words and said to Keller: "That's just what I came in for." He thanked Keller and left.

Alger Hiss was convicted on espionage-related perjury charges and served forty-four months of a five-year sentence in prison. Hiss' most recent attempt to clear his name by moving for a retrial was denied by a Federal judge.[1]

Another former Communist who received encouragement from Keller was Dr. Bella Dodd, a lawyer who had become actively involved with the Communist party in 1932. She joined the Teachers' Union in 1935 and promoted the party's interests in the New York State Federation of Teachers for the next nine years. In 1944, she became the first woman member of the party's top governing body, the National Committee, where she served until her resignation in 1948. According to her testimony before a Senate internal security subcommittee, she had helped set up Communist party cells in New York City colleges and in a number of prestigious universities in the East. Her defection from the party and return to Catholicism resulted from a meeting with Fulton Sheen in 1949.

The manner in which Keller met Dr. Dodd is not known, but in July 1952 she sent a small donation to the Christophers, noting that an issue of News Notes he had sent her provided the basis for a lively discussion among a group of union members in a Long Island aircraft plant. In her letter, she added: "I hope in time to be able to repay in a small measure for the strength and inspiration you transmitted to me at a time when faith and hope were almost extinguished." After her expulsion from the Communist party in 1949, Bella Dodd lost most of her lucrative law practice and was subjected to much harassment.

Keller's opposition to Communism was shaped both by patriotism and by his Catholicism. The Cold War that followed the

Soviet military takeover of Eastern Europe in the late 1940s ushered in a period of East-West military tensions that has continued, with minor interruptions, to the present.

Revelations of Soviet espionage divided Americans over the best way to counteract this threat. In his writings and speeches, Keller continually urged his hearers to promote the democratic and religious values by which they lived rather than concentrate exclusively on what they were against. This was perhaps his greatest contribution to the acrimonious debate over Communism.

If Keller's American instincts made him oppose Communism, his Catholic roots intensified this opposition. As long ago as 1848, Pope Pius IX had condemned "this evil doctrine which is called Communism" and the popes who followed him were equally unequivocal in their opposition to Marxian thought, particularly as expressed in the Soviet Union. Not until John XXIII became pope in 1958, did the Church's attitude toward Communism show a more nuanced appreciation of the wide diversity of those who embraced socialism. In his opening address to the Fathers of the Vatican Council (1962) Pope John said: "Nowadays . . . the Spouse of Christ prefers to make use of the medicine of mercy rather than that of severity. She concedes that she meets the needs of the present day by demonstrating the validity of her teaching rather than by condemnations." Though the two men never met, Keller would have been much more at home with John than with any of his predecessors over the previous century. Many people at the time of Vatican II remarked that Keller had anticipated the positive (or "pastoral") approach of that body by nearly thirty years. He never denied it.

For all his positive sentiments, Keller's language in the early days of the Christophers had an apocalyptic tinge. In August 1949, he wrote to the Maryknoll Council:

> The more I move around the country, the more convinced I become that we are all just a few jumps ahead of a terrible catastrophe. The forces of evil are sinking their roots in every place that will count when the crisis comes, and the vast majority of good people are scarcely aware of what is taking place under their very noses.

The "terrible catastrophe" Keller feared was the internal collapse of the United States, aided and abetted by Communists within and without. When the collapse did not come about, Keller had the good sense to back away from this line of thought. He would not be the first prophet to see his dire predictions fail to materialize. In his case, at least, it was with a sense of relief. He later admitted to a friend[2] that he had gone overboard in his anti-Communism. One of the public statements he most regretted was his reference in a speech to Communists as "rats." When a listener rebuked him for this, he quickly admitted his mistake. More often he was in tune with Pope John's sentiments: "A man who falls into error does not cease to be a man" (*Pacem in Terris*, 1963).

For all its denial of religious and political freedom, Communism fascinated Keller because of its power to inspire its millions of followers to heights of heroism. He saw Christians leading self-centered lives, unconcerned with the great issues swirling around them, while Communists led lives of austerity to bring about social justice. He was familiar with words such as those spoken by William Z. Foster, head of the U.S. Communist party, in 1937, about the penetration of the union movement:

> It is not enough to support the C.I.O. . . . . We must become leaders in these movements. We will then march forward with great strides in the revolutionary movement that is growing like a snowball in all parts of the United States.[3]

Keller was aware that American Communists had started "a new effective lay missionary program of their own." This was a reference to a nationwide string of adult training schools whose purpose and direction were, as he saw it, to undermine and overthrow the country he loved. He cited the Communist *Daily Worker* of January 3, 1949, in which the paper boasted that one of these institutions, the Jefferson School of Social Science in New York, had trained 50,000 people. At the urging of Archbishop McNicholas, Keller had several of the Christopher staff take courses at the Jefferson School at 16th Street and Sixth Avenue. What they learned was summarized by Keller in a quote he often used:

> What we give you doesn't belong to you alone. Get out and spread it. Don't take any kind of a job. Take only a job that

counts, a job where you can reach the many, not merely the few. Let the rest of the people take the ordinary jobs. Get on the staff of a college, on a board of education, in a government office, in a labor union, on a newspaper, into a television station, into the writing of comic books, or any other key spot where you can reach millions.[4]

In a rare foray into politics, Keller wrote an issue of News Notes advocating a letter-writing campaign to keep Communist China out of the United Nations. Its title mirrored the overheated atmosphere of the period: "Save the Orient—Write the President Now." According to the *Washington Daily News* (November 17, 1949), hundreds of thousands of letters poured into the nation's capital opposing any kind of recognition of the newly triumphant regime in China. Other groups were undoubtedly responsible for many of the letters, but the Christophers increased the total substantially. On another occasion, Keller sponsored a write-in to prevent the removal of J. Edgar Hoover as head of the Federal Bureau of Investigation. On the question of Senator Joseph McCarthy, whose witch-hunting tactics created more heat than light, Keller took no action either pro or con.

The Jefferson School provided Keller with his cue. If there were thirty-seven pro-Communist training schools across the country, he would set out to establish fifty Christopher Career Guidance Schools. His friend, Father Philip Carey, a Jesuit who conducted the Xavier Labor School, close by its Communist rival on 16th Street in New York, also served as an example. Nor was Carey's school unique. Max Kampelman, a specialist on Communist penetration of the labor movement,[5] estimated that one hundred Catholic labor schools had been established since the 1930s. Their course of study was intensely practical: labor law, contract negotiation, parliamentary procedure, economics, public speaking, and labor ethics. Experienced trade unionists taught many courses. Kampelman estimated that these schools enrolled 7,500 men and women each year, a number of whom assumed positions of leadership in the labor movement.

Why, it must be asked, did Keller want to start schools of his own? Wasn't he in danger of duplicating what others had done? On the contrary; what Keller had in mind was not another series of labor schools, but schools that would give would-be Christophers an introduction to fields he considered vital. Among them, he included college teaching, government work, writing in all its forms, social work, secretarial work, television, and motion pictures. Four to eight lectures on any subject, he felt, would be enough to give an interested person a taste for what was entailed in any given career.

In January 1949, Keller asked Bishop Lane of Maryknoll for approval to approach Cardinal Spellman for permission to start a Christopher Career Guidance School in New York. The approach was made, but the cardinal seems not to have responded, at least in writing. A few months later, Keller sent Lane the names of ten members of the hierarchy who approved of the school plan. Spellman's name was not among them.

The control of each school, according to Keller's plan, would be in the hands of the local Catholic bishop, whose priest-delegate would run it. The classes, to be held in the evening or on Saturdays in rented or donated building space, would be open to people of all faiths. As for finances, Keller estimated that $60,000 would be needed to get each school off the ground in its first year and that from then on it would be self-supporting.

Bishop Lane expressed cautious approval:

> The Council approves on principle the Christopher School project as you have outlined it. We should like, however, a written statement from you, which we can incorporate in our minutes, showing how it is to be organized, controlled and directed. This should be short, but sufficient.
>
> Likewise we should like to have your explanation of the measures to be taken to see that responsibility for errors or failures in the conduct of such schools does not fall upon you, and finally on Maryknoll.

With this much leeway, Keller hurried to get into print a twenty-two-page pamphlet called "Late—But Not Too Late." A few weeks later, Lane asked Keller to delay the publication. Keller assuaged his fears by changing the name from Christopher Career Guidance Schools to "Career Guidance Schools with a Christopher purpose." In a meeting with Lane that summer, Keller was forced to admit that his staff was inadequate to control the large sums of money needed to run the project. The Maryknoll Council had been shocked to learn that running fifty schools, with $60,000 in start-up moneys, would cost the Christophers $3 million—a sum larger than Maryknoll's entire budget. Keller agreed that something would have to be done to improve financial controls.

In his eagerness to save the country from Communism and to promote the Christopher idea through the school plan, Keller had stumbled on the question of money. As the Maryknoll Council looked more closely at the finances of Keller's school project—and the $1 million he was simultaneously trying to raise to make thirty films to be used as instructional guides—the dollar signs became so many stop signs. Thomas S. Walsh, a Council member, raised a warning flag in this memo to Lane:

> It is becoming increasingly obvious to me that Father Keller's genius lies almost exclusively in the field of promotion and not in that of originating ideas, nor in organizing, executing and administering a program. He started out with an idea, the 100 million, and then allowed himself to get pretty much diverted into something else, anti-Communism. Most of his financial support derives from the fact that he did get diverted into the struggle against Communism, but American public opinion is such that, in another year or two, the whole anti-Communist crusade could be so much "cold turkey" and a drug on the market. . . . The Council as a whole may want to approve Father Keller's proposal, but in doing so it should look ahead and try to foresee as well as possible the consequences. I as an individual member of the Council cannot approve and will want to go on record to that effect.

The status of the schools remained up in the air during the fall of 1949, though Keller did go ahead with the publication of 160,000 copies of "Late—But Not Too Late." Moreover, career guidance schools actually began in New York, Detroit, and Providence. Keller remained optimistic until a meeting with the Maryknoll authorities in late December of that year. His diary for the week recorded:

> Meeting at Maryknoll with Father General and the Council re: revised policy for control of Christopher work. New restrictions cut down the field a bit, but feel it is best to make an honest

try of them and so don't propose a single modification of the rules, even though Father General and Council invited discussion and offered changes if they felt that reasons submitted justified them.

At that meeting, Lane met Keller with a copy of the *Denver Register*[6] in his hand. It carried an eight-column headline about a $3 million budget for Christopher schools. Lane told Keller he wanted him to take a half-hour to think about dropping the idea of the career guidance schools. Keller replied: "I don't need a half-hour to think it over. If that's what you want me to do, I'll do it." The Council was amazed.

The restrictions did more than "cut down the field a bit," in Keller's optimistic phrase. They slammed the door on his dream of a nationwide network of career guidance schools—and probably saved him from endless fund-raising and management problems. Keller hid his disappointment, later admitting that Maryknoll had done him a favor. The new rules prevented Keller from seeking any funding for the schools, protected Maryknoll from any Christopher financial loss, and required that he receive approval in writing for any future Christopher program, project, or piece of literature. Finally, it laid down that a priest-representative cover the Christopher office in his absence. Either Keller had to get an assistant or give up his travels.

Keller had his eye on several priests who might help him. One was Father Thomas Bresnahan of Detroit, whom Keller had aided in the launching of a career guidance school that had been funded by the Detroit archdiocese. The project flourished, though it gradually narrowed its focus to "leadership," or public speaking. Under the title of the Gabriel Richard Institute,[7] the school continues to the present.

Other schools, also locally financed and directed, started in St. Paul, Buffalo, and probably in Spokane and Houston. But Keller's biggest find was a young priest who started a school in Providence at the end of 1949. Edward Flannery so impressed Keller that the latter asked Bishop Russell McVinney for his services at the Christopher office in New York. Flannery was released and spent the next five years commuting to New York for weekdays and returning home for parish work on weekends. This left Keller free to roam the country.

Flannery had a meditative, scholarly mind. He subscribed to Keller's general views, but was less apt to be carried away by enthusiasms of the moment. He did a good deal of research on Christopher books, especially a volume on the public schools called *All God's Children*.

Flannery's feelings about Keller and his work were expressed in this letter:

> He [Keller] had a firm conviction of having a very serious mission in life, and who can deny that he had? He often spoke of the "work" in reverential tones, and he had a sense that God was always in support of what he did. I didn't care too much for the way he mixed the "Communist threat" with his promotional efforts. Some of his respondents actually saw this as a "scare technique," frightening people into believing that they would lose all their money with a Communist takeover. Jim was sincerely and perhaps overly anti-Communist, and he was a master-fundraiser, and at times both of these got slightly mixed together. I say this in face of the fact that I always admired Jim and affirmed his work.[8]

Flannery returned to his home diocese in 1955, where he became deeply involved in Christian-Jewish relations. His book, *The Anguish of the Jews*, was well received by Jewish organizations, and he became an advisor to the U.S. Catholic bishops on the subject.

Relieved of some of his work by Flannery's arrival, Keller pushed ahead with the career book during 1950. His diary for June stated:

> Have been trying to sandwich in work on a second book called *Careers That Count*. Had originally planned it for next year, but due to the urgency of getting people into the vital fields without delay, I feel we should rush this. Many people in Washington are helping us on the chapter on Federal Government. Here was an interesting sidelight: the head of personnel of the State Department told us that at no time do they have enough people applying to fill the jobs that are open. I often wonder if China might not have been saved if we had done a little missionary work along these lines ten years ago.

Keller and his associates, Joseph Calderon, Jane Harris, and Charles Oxton, wrote and rewrote the chapters through the summer.[9] A hardcover printing was accompanied by two paperback printings of 100,000 each.

With his facility for turning obstacles into opportunities, Keller made the book a substitute for, instead of an accompaniment to, the career guidance schools. In his News Notes for April 1951 (#34), he announced:

> Our Christopher objective of 5000 informal career guidance schools or study clubs is forging ahead in many sections of the country. Anyone can set up one of these schools in a family, club, college, high school, service group or any legitimate organization. We feel it sensible and practical to use existing institutions, rather than set up something entirely new.
>
> As few as 5 or 10 persons can make up a career guidance school of their own, choose a leader from their midst, and use our latest Christopher book, *Careers That Change Your World* as a basic text.

The career book did not achieve the popularity of *You Can Change the World*, but it turned the minds of many readers toward the idea of getting a job in "a field that counts." Except for the Communists, hardly anyone else was talking in this way in 1950. The effect of the book on one young lawyer is shown in this letter (4/22/52):

> I am a 1951 graduate of the University of Notre Dame Law School. I have been practicing in Garrett, Indiana, for four months, am married and the father of a year-old-boy.
>
> I, like so many others, have avoided entering politics for the reason that it seemed impossible to do so and still keep some semblance of moral integrity. However, your book on career guidance has inspired me to do what I can in this direction. I am going to run for County Prosecutor next fall. It is a small job, but may give me a chance to do some good.

Keller's preoccupation with Communism gradually faded, and there was less mention of the subject in his books and other literature. He became more absorbed in the factors that made people "tick"—that led them to decide to make something of their lives. "What one person can do" fascinated him throughout his life.

Keller's last major treatment of Communism took the form of a 1962 News Note (#119), "Seven Ways to Overcome Communism." Against the background of the Cuban missile crisis and Khrushchev's fulminations at the United Nations, it was a great success. More than one million reprints were ordered by readers; it was translated into Spanish; and it was even distributed throughout Mexico in comic book form. Typical of the affirmative nature of this publication was this recognition that social injustice played a large part in the growth of Communist influence:

> Those living in poverty and misery are not impressed when Christians wait until there is a Communist threat before coming to their assistance. They interpret this more as self-interest than as a desire to help Christ's poor.

Keller was well aware that extreme right-wingers used the anti-Communist cry to prevent meaningful change. He also knew that the failure of Christians to live up to the practical consequences of their faith left a vacuum in which agitators of all kinds could cause trouble. The difference between the older and the younger James Keller was that, as he aged, he seemed more responsive to the need for social justice for its own sake.

The Keller children in 1905: *rear* (*left to right*):
Hazel and Harold; *front*: James, Reginald, and Louis.

The Keller family on the day of James's ordination,
August 15, 1925: (*left to right*) Hazel, Louis, Mrs. Keller,
James, Mr. Keller, Mildred, and Reginald.

with Bishop
Anthony Walsh,
knoll's cofounder.
en them
her Jepson,
ician.

Henry Ford, in the white suit, with Keller at the wedding reception
for Henry Ford II and Anne McDonnell, Southampton, July 1940.

Loretta Young accepting Christopher Award on behalf
of Mervyn LeRoy, February 1952.

Jeanne Glynn and Jack Denove confer with Keller in 1957
TV filming.

Keller interviews Dr. Howard A. Rusk, international expert on rehabilitation medicine.

A break for prayer during interlude in TV filming.

Terence Cardinal Cooke presenting Keller with papal award
in January 1976. *Standing (left to right)*: Fred Sauter,
Jeanne Glynn, Richard Armstrong, Dolores Criqui, and
William Wilson of the Christophers.

•*12*•

Criticism from Within

"Anybody would be justified in criticizing us personally.
We have many defects, more limitations. All we strive to
be is an errand-boy of Christ—to bring Christ's love where
there is hatred, his light where there is darkness."

James Keller

For ten years, Keller fiddled with an idea for a book of daily meditations that could be used by people too busy to settle down to any formal method of prayer. Beginning in 1940, he tried various approaches, showing each of them to a number of friends, but without striking the right chord. Some showed surprise that he kept at it despite many unsuccessful attempts, but Keller was a determined man.

At first he tried opening each meditation with a quotation from the Bible. This seemed to turn off people who weren't particularly religious. Then he started with a general ethical reflection, but this sounded too preachy. Finally, he used a human interest story, usually some incident he had read in and clipped from a newspaper. Having thus captured his readers' interest, he could make a transition to the "moral" and add a prayer and biblical quotation. That seemed to work. After all, Christ taught in parables.

Peter Grace was one of those to whom Keller used to send his meditations, and this had an unexpected corollary. Grace's secretary, Margaret Fennelly, was impressed by the fact that her boss read such "spiritual literature," and so when Grace proposed marriage to her, she had no hesitation about accepting.

The book that grew out of the meditations was called *Three Min-*

utes a Day and was published by Doubleday in 1949. It was promoted heavily in newspapers and magazines, and Keller made appearances at autographing sessions in department and book stores across the country. The hardcover edition sold 170,000 copies and was later brought out in paperback. The simple, brief stories with a spiritual twist and Scripture passage—one for each day of the year—proved once again that Keller was at his best devising formulas that would appeal to "the man in the street."

Columnist Bob Considine plugged the book by "the dynamic Maryknoll missionary whose Christopher movement has quickened in hundreds of thousands of Americans a fresh zeal to live better lives":

> *Three Minutes a Day* is broken into 365 short chapters, each an anecdote—superbly told—dealing with the inherent goodness of the human being, regardless of his religion, color and estate. Under each is a short, fitting prayer. Each chapter takes three minutes to read, but the thoughts engendered will last a lifetime in the hearts of its readers.

The Bell Syndicate featured daily thoughts from *Three Minutes a Day* in several dozen newspapers, but the book contained only a year's supply. In a phrase he often used, Keller had "a tiger by the tail." To keep the column going, he had to continue to supply new meditations. He wrote these reflections everywhere—on trains, in airplanes, aboard ocean liners, or after-hours in his office. His office staff clipped "filler" stories from newspapers to provide material for the meditations, but the burden of writing them was his. It would be years before he would find an assistant to write "three minutes a day" to his satisfaction.

In 1950, a second volume followed, called *One Moment, Please.*

Several years later, the McNaught Syndicate took over the distribution of the newspaper column and the number of subscribing papers reached a high point of 103 in 1963, by which time Keller had produced fourteen meditation books.

One of the priest's favorite proverbs became the basis for a three-minute meditation which began: " 'The dogs bark, but the caravan moves on' is an age-old proverb that has a valuable lesson for those bothered by unfair criticism." It concluded: "Be true to God, to yourself and to others in pursuing your mission in life and no amount of criticism will ever dissuade you, much less stop you."

Keller followed his own advice. Rarely did he respond to criticism in the pursuit of his mission. If he did, it was in a way that forced his critics to examine their motives, if not their facts. The only exception was disapproval from religious authorities, which he took with great seriousness. There were times when he must have thought that people in his own Maryknoll society were trying to sidetrack his "caravan." In 1948, Keller's Christopher staff was getting so big that it disrupted the office procedure of the Maryknoll workers at the New York house. Word came from Maryknoll to move the Christopher office to a more inconspicuous part of the building. Walter Maxcy recalled the occasion:

> One time I saw him a little depressed when the Christophers were moved from the third floor to the first floor [at 39th Street], the street level. He was told to do this by Maryknoll and, of course, he did so, although he saw the handwriting on the wall. [He said,] "The next step is out the front door"—and it was.

In April 1949, Keller resigned as head of the Maryknoll operation. A few months later, he rented office space in the Great Lakes Carbon Building on 48th Street, which was offered to him by the Skakel family, the owner of the building. That Patricia Skakel, whose sister Ethel was to marry Robert Kennedy, was working for the Christophers at the time was no doubt a factor in obtaining this new space.

Nevertheless, Keller continued to live at the 39th Street house of Maryknoll where he took part in spiritual exercises and meals when he was in the city, although he did not often socialize with the other priests. There was always "the work"—his mission—to attend to. Maryknoll's Promotion Department, however, had no intention of allowing him to regain a foothold on 39th Street. Such was its relief, when the Christopher workers were finally gone, that Keller's attempt to do some weekend work there was rebuffed. The rather pathetic incident is contained in this letter Keller wrote to his successor and one-time assistant, Joseph English, on Christmas Day, 1950:

Dear Joe:

When I was up at Maryknoll on Saturday, I told Father General about my hope to get out three books this year if I can cut out some routine work and find a quiet corner to push ahead with each of them. Because of many distractions, it is not possible to get much done at the Christopher office in the way of writing. And finding any other suitable spot in a rectory or private home for continuous work is close to impossible.

So I asked Father General if it would be okay for an assistant and myself to use any spot on the first floor here for the writing. I told him it would be ideal. He gave a warm approval and suggested using the little room at the rear, if it met with your okay.

If you approve, Joe, it would be a big help. If the small room is not available for this work, you may think of another corner that you would see fit to loan for this purpose.

English did not approve. He was backed by McCarthy, so Keller's request for a *pied à terre* was turned down. A small incident, but it gives an indication of the strained atmosphere.

Keller looked in vain for some sign of approval of his work in *The Field Afar*, whose large circulation would have been beneficial to his mission. It was McCarthy's decision to make, but Keller went over his head directly to Lane. In July 1950, he wrote to the Superior General:

If you and the Council see fit to run something in the F. A. [*Field Afar*] in the next several months on the Christophers being directed by a Maryknoller, while stressing the distinction from the Society, I think it would clear up better than any other move the impression that Maryknoll is not too enthused re: the Christophers, which is quite contrary to all the generous help that you and the Council and most of our men have shown. While this impression exists only among a few, yet the fact that Maryknoll has made no public reference to the Christophers might help spread this view. On the other [hand], one tactful, brief item could easily dispel any such notion. But you will know best on this.

As luck would have it, Lane was away and the matter was referred to McCarthy, whom Keller was probably trying to circumvent. McCarthy vented his feelings in this internal memorandum:

I do not favor mentioning the Christophers in the F. A. It is not Maryknoll work, it is not foreign mission work. The F. A. is for our Cause, of which the Christophers are not a part. In my calculations of Promotion receipts, the Christophers have cost us a half million dollars, minimum. I do not favor Maryknoll's mentioning the Christophers.

Even Considine, Keller's close friend and collaborator from the thirties, closed ranks with McCarthy, though mainly to preserve a united front. In his memo, he said:

I would like to stand with Father McCarthy on such matters since it is important that he take the lead in fixing policy. He tells me he is categorically opposed to any mention of the Christophers. I regret this for several reasons:

1. I think there is a certain confusion in the minds of many friends that could be cleared up by a word of explanation and that such clarification is as important for us as for the Christophers.

2. I think that we should avoid any indication of sullenness and ill will toward the Christopher movement. Such an attitude can only cause scandal and bring us discredit. Calculating silence can be as harmful in this respect as is loose talk. True, theoretically it has cost us a half a million dollars that Father Keller would have turned into Maryknoll had he stayed at his old job. I don't think we gain anything, however, by revealing our displeasure even negatively.

3. Despite all its fine points, the Christopher movement may prove short-lived and Father Keller may be prepared sooner than we suspect to take up work again with us. I think it will be unfortunate if we have marked this period by unnecessary refusals to cooperate with him.

4. I think it is unhealthy for members of the Society to note that Society officials assume a chilly and sour attitude toward a project such as this.

Rather than make matters worse, Keller cut his losses and made this bare acknowledgment to Bishop Lane: "Thanks so much for your thoughtful letter re: any reference to the Christophers in the F. A." It would be twenty years before Maryknoll's large circulation magazine took any notice of the Christophers.

Why this grudging attitude toward a man who had done so much for his society and who, at the time, was one of the most popular priests in America? Part of the reason can be attributed to jealousy, which exists in religious societies as elsewhere. Part arose from a genuine conviction that Keller should have devoted himself exclusively to Maryknoll work. And part can be traced to Keller's own attitude, which betrayed a certain insensitivity to the feelings of other Maryknollers. Many Maryknoll promoters were still upset by Keller's actions at the time of a large retreat and strategy meeting of priests from that department in Brookline, Massachusetts, during the summer of 1949. Keller declined an invitation to be present, citing the fact that he needed a rest and would be in Maine at that time. Instead of attending, he sent a long paper, which, at his request, was read to the assembled promoters.

McCarthy had the paper reproduced and distributed at the meeting. To it, he appended these remarks:

> The views expressed are strictly Father Keller's own. The first reaction of some will be irritation, but there is a challenge in these thoughts that will stir many to greater effort.
>
> Some of the statements may not be true, some of the ideas may be contrary to our traditions, but if so, they are the fault of great zeal on Father Keller's part and not of ill intent. Freedom of expression is an American institution and the expression of views contrary to our own is a challenge which stimulates thought and progress.
>
> Though I do not agree with all of Father Keller's statements since I know that some of them are contrary to fact, particularly in regard to Members of our faculties and the Public Relations Department (I don't think that he is referring to missioners on the field), yet I believe that he offers a challenge that we should face squarely.

The title of the eight-page paper, "If We Won't, Who Will?" read like an issue of the Christopher News Notes. Keller began by reminding his audience that the Christian portion of the world's 2.3 billion population was shrinking, while the numbers of those coming under the domination of Communism was growing. He gave the examples of Maryknoll's cofounders, Father Price and

Bishop Walsh, as men whose vision went far beyond Maryknoll and embraced the entire world. Then he asked:

> Isn't the mission of Maryknoll a far more lofty one than merely taking care of Maryknoll? Are we slipping into mediocrity, becoming just another society? What does our Lord expect of us? What has the Church a right to expect of us? . . . If we permit this apparent trend to continue—over-emphasizing Maryknoll, underemphasizing winning the world for Christ— I fear we shall pay the penalty. . . . Finding vocations and financial support will become more and more difficult in proportion as we diminish Maryknoll's vision in our own minds and in the minds of the people.

Keller recommended that Maryknoll promoters set a goal of preparing one thousand priests a year to go out over the world. If that was too much for Maryknoll alone, then he suggested: "If ten societies are needed to provide 1,000 new priests, let's stir up ten old societies or keep pushing for ten new ones. Let us further propose that the first step in financing this would be to raise $15 million for the first eight or ten of these seminaries."

His paper concluded with several questions:

> Isn't it possible that this inbreeding on the part of the followers of Christ is more responsible for the present mess than what the missioners of evil are doing? Aren't we tending to be a protective society, or a sect, rather than fully Catholic?—missing the forest for the trees?—overcautious from a human point of view?—are we too close to what we are doing to appreciate what we are not doing? . . . Will we pitch in before it is too late? That is up to each of us. If we don't, Maryknoll may soon suffer the same fate that has crippled most of the mission societies of Europe. And worse still, our Church, our country and our world may be plunged into the worst nightmare that has yet visited mankind.

Some of the priests at the Brookline meeting supported Keller's visionary paper and others opposed it. A session was held on Friday night, June 17, to weigh all reactions and to draft a formal reply. This was sent to Keller in California, where he had gone to work on television programs. (His vacation in Maine had somehow been skipped.)

On the basis of informal minutes taken by Father James Courneen, the meeting itself went this way:

> The feeling had been high since the night previous and, since it was quite obvious that no calm progress could be made immediately after the reading of [Keller's] paper by Father Haren, the discussion was left until Friday night, after thoughts could be gathered and clarified. . . . There were some promoters, or perhaps just one, who thought the criticism of Maryknoll in the paper was completely unjust and should be answered. . . . Others said that the criticism ought to be thrown aside, whether unjustified or not, and instead the good constructive thoughts be considered. . . . Some were insulted by the paper and confused by its claims. Others were not and thought that the paper had many worthwhile merits. Generally, though, the criticism of Maryknoll was not favorably received. . . . So concluded these meetings at Brookline in a spirit of prayer, peace and calm.

In their formal reply, the promoters, after disagreeing with Keller's interpretation of the words of Bishop Walsh, the cofounder, about the evangelization of the world, continued:

> We feel that we ought to get the best out of whatever Father Keller says. We believe his letter should cause us to aim higher and, although his criticism of us may tend to distract us from his constructive suggestions, we ought to be big enough to draw good out of it.

The two-page letter, which did not discuss the substantive points raised by Keller, concluded with a reference to Keller's call that Maryknollers do something to "save the world," not merely Maryknoll:

> We agree with Father Keller on world vision—we disagree with the suggestion that we are doing our work only in our own sphere. Foreign Missions is our contribution to the world vision. The Holy See, for example, has told us not to do Negro work

in the U.S.A.[1] The Cardinal of Chicago has said that Mary-knoll always will have the support of the hierarchy if it sticks to its own work and purpose. The promoters feel that they can help change the world without changing the policy of Mary-knoll.

Bishop Lane asked McCarthy to cite instances of confusion aris-ing in the minds of clergy and laity over the relationship between Maryknoll and the Christophers. McCarthy said that there was uncertainty at the New York house as to whether certain gifts were designated for one or the other. He gave three examples from the experience of Father Norbert Rans in St. Paul, in which it was alleged that money intended for Maryknoll went to the Christo-phers. McCarthy expressed his opinion that donations to the Chris-tophers did not really come out of Maryknoll's pockets in any big way. He said:

> The real competition that cuts into a Church or a charity is not another charity, but the luxuries such as liquor, cars, gambling, etc., that take money out of the pockets of so many people and leave them nothing to give to charity. I do not think that, in the long run, the Christophers will hurt Maryknoll. In fact, they would not hurt us at all if the founder and director were not a Maryknoller.

In a memo to the Maryknoll Council, T. S. Walsh, the vicar general, warned: "This affair may have the makings of a dangerous internal controversy and, for that reason, we should be careful about the manner in which we handle it."

Since Keller had not himself appeared at the Brookline meeting to observe the reactions of his hearers and answer questions on the spot, the whole matter revolved around Maryknoll versus the Chris-tophers, rather than Maryknoll's future direction. In Keller's paper, the Christopher movement was not even mentioned. His absence had put him on the defensive. After hearing from a number of promoters, Keller wrote to Father James McDermott in Los Angeles elaborating on his paper and listing the advantages to Maryknoll of Christopher work. He went on at some length about the efforts he had made to keep Maryknoll benefactors from switching their sup-port to the Christophers. McDermott was satisfied. He wrote:

Thanks a million! I read—and will re-read—your July 14th communications. I feel "humbled"—I hope you sent a copy of these to every promoter. As I told the Fathers, I try to boost the Christopher movement everytime. And I am proud that it was a Maryknoll Father who established the Christophers. More power to you, Jim. If only Father General issued your challenge!!! I guess there are some of us who are too small—and who resent Father Jim Keller—God forgive us. From now on, Jim, I'll remember the Christopher movement in my Mass and prayers.

Lane, who had been away part of the time, remained above the fray. At the end of July, he wrote Keller about the "tempest in a teapot," requesting a meeting to clarify certain things and telling him that now he (Lane) would be forced to put out some clarifying statement.

The meeting was held late in August 1949. Lane gave his account of what happened:

> I told him that I thought he had made a mistake in the letter that he had written to be read at Brookline. At first, he did not seem anxious to admit this, but after some discussion and after hearing the reasons I gave for my statement, he admitted that possibly it was a mistake. I told him I thought it was the most serious one he had made since he took over the Christophers, particularly since it was connected with his not making the retreat with our men. . . . This seemed to surprise him, but he realized afterwards that it was rather thoughtless of him. . . . I then got back again to the question of the Brookline business and told him that the whole matter could have led to an unfortunate division in the Society, namely the pro-Kellerites and the anti-Kellerites. . . . He admitted all of this, and I think that he saw clearly before the end that he had been imprudent and had gotten away from our community in a certain sense.

The "tempest" remained confined to the Maryknoll "teapot." Following the guidelines listed in the previous chapter, Keller remained under the wing of Maryknoll and the Christophers operated with relative liberty. The move from 39th Street to the new Christopher offices at 48th Street helped. Eventually, Cardinal Spellman set up a committee, consisting of three New York auxiliary bishops and T. S. Walsh, to meet with Keller quarterly for a review of finances and major activities. What could have become an explosive situation was effectively defused, leaving James Keller free to turn his attention to more exciting pursuits.

•13•

A Pat on the Back

"The pat went clear to my soul."
Lee Cooley, Television Producer

One of the most penetrating and enduring effects of the Christopher movement is the awards given each year to producers, directors, and writers. Although the awards cover virtually every aspect of the mass media, the original idea of James Keller was to honor a theatrical production.

As early as 1947, Keller got in touch with James Cardinal McIntyre of Los Angeles, saying he planned to give $10,000 in prize money to the three Broadway plays that best upheld Christian principles. It was not until April 27, 1949, however, that the first award winners were announced. Meanwhile, the concept had expanded to include books and motion pictures, and the financial rewards of the contest increased accordingly. "For the Christopher Awards," said Keller, "we decided to offer the largest literary prize ever given—up until then the highest had been $20,000. We decided to give $25,000! And then, in bed one night, I decided that was too little . . . so I changed it to $30,000."[1]

The contest was announced in several issues of Christopher News Notes and received nationwide publicity through articles in *Time* and *Newsweek*. Under the headline "Calling All Christophers" (4/-14/47), *Time* had this to say:

> Father Keller's Christophers made news last week that will be heard even in such secular strongholds as the offices of authors' agents and cinemoguls. They announced a prize book contest

baited with enough cash to make big league authors sit up and take notice—$15,000 for the first prize, $10,000 for the second, and $5,000 for the third. With all rights to remain with the authors. Manuscripts (to be submitted by November 15, 1948) may be fiction, biographies, or whodunits; the only stipulation is "that they be in accordance with Christian principles and not against them." Book publishers and movie makers have told Father Keller that they are hungry for just the kind of plain Christian writing the Christophers' contest is designed to produce.

The response was enormous. Nearly 2,500 books and manuscripts poured in from every state in the union, Canada, and a dozen other countries. Of that number, 1,102 came from women, 483 of whom were married. Catholic priests contributed 37 manuscripts, 23 came from Protestant ministers, and 17 entries were sent by doctors. For sheer quantity, the record was set by a woman who entered 5 plays and 4 novels. New Yorkers sent in 340 manuscripts and California was second with 295, followed by Ohio, 83; Pennsylvania, 74; Illinois, 72; while Massachusetts and Texas were tied with 68. Bob Considine quipped, "This is believed to be the first time Texas ever finished out of the money in any field of endeavor."

The avalanche of literary outpourings kept a screening staff buried under manuscripts for many months, as they looked for promising entries to submit to the judges. Clare Boothe Luce, Fulton Oursler, Mary O'Hara, and Father John S. Kennedy judged the books. Judges of dramatic works were Katharine Cornell, Eddie Dowling, Oscar Hammerstein II, Leo McCarey, and Jo Mielziner.

At a luncheon held at the Commodore Hotel in New York City, on April 27, 1949, the award winners were announced. First prize in the book category went to George Howe, a Washington architect, for his novel, *Call It Treason*, a spy thriller. It was published by Viking and was made into the motion picture, *Decision before Dawn*. Howe, a World War II veteran who had been with the OSS in Africa and France, had made several false starts on writing a novel. While he was confined to a hospital bed with injuries from an automobile accident, his sister told him about the Christopher contest. "I doubt if I could have stuck to writing my book with a leg and jaw in traction," he said, "except for the inspiration of the contest."

Second prize went to Marie Nowinson of Chicago for her book, *The Martels*, the story of an unsuccessful lawyer who buried his dreams in a life of sacrifice for his children. Third prize was awarded to Charles O'Neal of Hollywood, who described his novel, *Three Wishes*, as a "light Irish story, rather whimsical."

In the field of drama, the $5,000 award was given to Rosemary Casey of Pittsburgh, for her comedy, *Mother Hildebrand*, which opened at the Booth Theater in New York under the title, *The Velvet Glove*. It concerned the superior of a religious order who protected a liberal professor at her college from dismissal as a radical by sweetly threatening to sabotage the bishop's fund-raising plans. The performances of Grace George and Walter Hampden were highly praised, but the script itself was tagged "a sparse, skimpy but pleasant comedy" by the *New York Sun*. Brooks Atkinson of the *New York Times* concluded that the play was "not likely to promote Christian ideals in American living, nor to damage them very much."

The $3,000 second prize was given to John L. Oberg of Hollywood for his drama, *The Night and the Star*. Rounding out the award ceremonies was a $2,000 presentation to Father Urban Nagle of the Blackfriars' Guild for his play, *City of Kings*.

Keller soon had an opportunity to make a motion picture award, though he did so with misgivings. The picture of the year, from his point of view, was *Joan of Arc*, starring Ingrid Bergman. But Bergman had recently left her husband, Doctor Peter Lindstrom, and had gone to live with movie director Roberto Rossellini. Keller had met the actress in Rome in March 1948 and sought to persuade her to return to her husband. He also wrote to her twice, to no effect, and talked with Doctor Lindstrom in New York in hopes of effecting a reconciliation.

What tipped the scales in favor of the movie was a letter from Martin Quigley, publisher of the *Motion Picture Herald*. Quigley wrote (5/3/49):

Critically, I think the picture itself and Miss Bergman's personal behavior are two separate and distinct matters. I believe that it is faulty and dangerous reasoning to judge the moral status of the picture by either the good conduct or the bad conduct of a performer. Irrespective of Miss Bergman's personal life—about which we do not know much—she portrayed, effectively and movingly, the character on the screen. . . . If Catholics do not support pictures like *Joan of Arc*, there is no reason for them to be made.

Clearances were secured from the chancery offices in New York and Los Angeles and from the Legion of Decency. On May 30, 1949, the 418th anniversary of the death of the warrior-saint, the first Christopher motion picture award was announced. Producer, director, and writer were not cited. The movie itself was given the award.

Keller learned several things from the experience of making his first awards: (1) it was much too time-consuming to solicit manuscripts from unpublished authors; (2) the Broadway audience was too limited and plays too subject to nuances of interpretation; and (3) he could move more quickly if he had no "name" judges and relied instead on an informal network of advisors.

The 1950 Christopher Awards were announced in two different cities: the book awards at the Astor Hotel in New York, on February 15, 1951; and the film awards at the Ambassador Hotel in Los Angeles five days later. Each of the five winners received $5,000. Since it was no longer a contest, the three books were given equal billing. They were: *In Our Image*, with texts of the Bible selected by Houston Harte, a Texas journalist, and illustrations by Guy Rowe, an artist who did *Time* covers; *Pillar of Fire*, by Dr. Karl Stern, the story of a Jewish psychiatrist in Nazi Germany and his search for meaning in life; and *Miracle at Carville*, by Evelyn Wells and "Betty Martin," the pseudonym for a woman whose conquest of leprosy eventually led to her return to society.

In the motion picture field, *Cheaper by the Dozen*, the story of the Gilbreth family, and *Father of the Bride*, a domestic comedy, were chosen. Script writers only were singled out: Lamar Trotti for *Cheaper* and Frances Goodrich and Albert Hackett for *Father*. At the reception in Los Angeles, Keller said:

> The Hollywood script writer seldom gets the recognition he deserves in writing scripts that are at the same time entertaining, artistic and inspirational.

Thomas Merton, the Trappist monk of *Seven Storey Mountain* fame, sent a letter to Robert Giroux of Harcourt Brace, which was forwarded to the Christophers. In it, he said:

> Karl Stern's conversion would be the death of the nineteenth century myth that science and religion are incompatible, if that myth had not already died long ago. He not only shows that a scientific attitude of mind is no obstacle to faith, but that a scientist who is fully aware of the implications of his science is bound to accept faith. . . . Some day, I think, many people are going to follow the road that Dr. Stern has followed.

Karl Stern himself wrote to Keller from McGill University in Montreal, saying: "You simply cannot imagine the stir which this news created in this secular university here, particularly in its most materialistic circles. That a psychiatrist would win a Christian award!"

"Betty Martin" who had been living in a trailer in San Diego, used her portion of the prize money to purchase a home. The Hacketts wrote: "We accept it with gratitude to you, and to the many good people all over the country who have contributed to it. We are deeply touched and we feel a great sense of responsibility."

Donations by about 8,000 people had made the Christopher Award money possible.

Lamar Trotti, who had just lost one son in an auto accident and nearly lost another, donated his prize money to the University of Georgia, his alma mater, for a scholarship in memory of his son. He wrote:

> When you come out here, I hope to see you. I find it difficult, almost impossible, to talk to anyone, but I think I might to you if it will not burden you. . . . I have won several awards in my life, an Oscar among them, but none has given me the warm feeling of pride that this has.

The 1951 presentation, made on February 14, 1952, at the Beverly Hills Hotel, now included awards to television, "Amahl and the Night Visitors," the first opera written for TV; "The Path of Praise," the story of Sarah Hale and the Thanksgiving holiday; a news story in the Atlanta *Constitution* about a little girl who led other patrons in a lunchroom in prayer; and "See How They Run," an article in the *Ladies' Home Journal* about a teacher in the South who inspired her students.

Mary Elizabeth Vroman, the author of "See How They Run," was the first black person ever to enter the Beverly Hills Hotel as a guest. In her acceptance remarks, she said:

> When I wrote "See How They Run," it was with the primary aim . . . to develop a talent I believed I had, and secondly, to bring an awareness to the reading public of how boys and girls in a Negro school are identical with children everywhere— loveable, sometimes exasperating, and completely wonderful in their ability to grow like French weeds through the rocks of stiflingly infertile soil not of their own making.

More than 200 representatives of the mass communications media attended the awards dinner. The presentation was broadcast on the NBC radio network at 9:30 P.M., Pacific Standard Time.

Quo Vadis, the motion picture award, did create some controversy. Walter Kerr, then drama critic for *Commonweal*, found the film to be "an essay in calculated vulgarity." He thought the Christopher citation would give people the impression that "the 'Catholic' concept of art is a decidedly primitive one."

Without responding directly to Kerr, Keller replied to critics of *Quo Vadis* in an issue of News Notes titled, "Why the Christopher Awards?" He said:

> It is not easy to find works that conform to high standards in all respects. Some are strong in *content* but weak in *structure* or *form*. Others are exquisitely presented, but with a story that accents evil rather than good. . . . It is easy for all of us to find fault. But it requires both a Christlike head and heart to find the element of good in both the literary and entertainment fields and to build on that. . . . In most cases, awards and prizes alike encourage the recipient to reach greater heights. Awards would seldom, if ever, be given if made only to the perfect work.

Another critic was Dan Herr, writing in *Books on Trial*, a Catholic literary magazine. He was disturbed by the transition of the awards from a contest for new writers to "just another publicity contest awarding fat prizes to well-established authors whose products had already been accepted by the public."

The 1951 awards marked the last time that money was distributed. Henceforth, recipients were given a bronze medallion with the figures of St. Christopher and the Christ Child on one side and the Christopher motto: "Better to light one candle than to curse the darkness" on the other.

Christopher Awards continued until 1961, when they were discontinued because Keller found the task too burdensome. They were resumed in 1969, after his retirement.

Of the more than fifty book awards made during this ten-year period, about one-third went to well-known personalities, including Senator John F. Kennedy, J. Edgar Hoover, Charles Lindbergh, Anne Morrow Lindbergh, and Clare Boothe Luce. Journalist Jim Bishop received a special award in 1957 for his book *The Day Christ Died*.

Authors best known to Catholic audiences included Thomas Merton, Fulton Sheen, John Courtney Murray, S.J., and Jacques Maritain.

Maryknoller John Considine sent this word of gratitude for the award to his book *New Horizons in Latin America* (1958):

> Heartfelt thanks for the generous gesture in naming me among the great in the Christopher Catholic book awards. Father Nevins had occasion to drop in at Dodd, Mead Company and found Mr. Bons, the boss, very tickled over the letter you sent the firm. Apart from the personal kudos involved, the idea strikes me as a very good one for encouraging writers and publishers.

W.A. Swanberg, the biographer, who was cited for *First Blood— The Story of Fort Sumter* (1958), alluded to the modest form of presentation:

> I'm pleased as can be to learn that I am one of those cited for the Christopher Award. This award, which you describe modestly as "just a little pat on the back," has a warmth and meaning missing in some of the others.

Charles W. Ferguson, a senior editor at the *Reader's Digest*, also recognized the impact of the award:

I can't tell you how pleased and touched I am by your news that *Naked to Mine Enemies* will receive one of the Christopher awards. This means real recognition from persons who are very attentive to the contents of books and I appreciate the recognition deeply.

John Courtney Murray, the Jesuit whose advanced views on the role of the Catholic Church in the modern state decisively influenced Church teaching on religious liberty at the Second Vatican Council a few years later, thanked Keller for the Christopher Award to his book, *We Hold These Truths* (1961):

> The Christopher Award is indeed an undeserved honor. On the other hand, *valet illud Augustini: gratiam non propter merita dari* ["what Augustine said is true: grace is not given on account of merit"]. I want you to know of my appreciation. It was good to see you. May God our Lord further all your undertakings.

During this decade, the list of motion picture producers honored by the Christophers read like a "Who's Who" of Hollywood: Samuel Goldwyn, Walt Disney, Louis de Rochemont, and many others, as well as many of the best-known directors.

It gave Keller special pleasure to give an award to *Bright Road* (1953), because it was the screen version of Mary Elizabeth Vroman's award-winning magazine article "See How They Run." The first foreign films cited were *Pather Panchali* by the Indian filmmaker, Satyajit Ray, and a *A Night to Remember*, produced by the Rank organization.

Hollywood people knew that the Christopher Award was one prize for which it was not possible to lobby. Typical was a letter from Henry Koster, director of *Stars and Stripes Forever* (1952):

> The merit of an award is judged not only by the accomplishments of the recipient but even more by the standards of the group which makes the presentation. Therefore, I feel it is a particular honor to accept this award, since the Christophers are known for their dedication to the highest ideals in all art forms.

Scriptwriter Richard Simmons, who worked on *The Private War of Major Benson* (1955), showed what an award meant to him:

When one practices the entertainment arts by spinning yarns at a film studio typewriter, there is an unfortunate sense of working into a vacuum. A script is written, disappears onto a set and emerges as a film to amuse or torment an audience whom we rarely meet. Satisfaction, as you surely know, comes infrequently. . . . I cherish not only your plaque itself but the assurance that there are men such as you, organizations such as yours and, indeed, a considerable audience taking a hand in creative matters by creating for us an aspiration level toward which to extend whatever abilities we have.

Peter Viertel, who wrote the film script for *Old Man and the Sea* (1958) from Ernest Hemingway's book, showed his appreciation:

It was a wonderful and inspiring book and, if at least some of this comes out on the screen, I feel that the part I had in making the picture was worth the work involved. I know that it is not an "audience" picture in that rather doubtful sense of the word. In the long run, perhaps, it will be seen by a great many people, and the intent of the book will reach an even wider audience than it did in its literary form.

One of the few dissenting notes on Christopher film awards came from the editor of a Catholic paper in the South. Father Vincent Smith of the *Florida Catholic*, relying on a review in *Time*, criticized the Christophers for their award to *Good Heavens, Mr. Allison*. His editorial was captioned: "Film Industry Profanes Our Sisters."

Keller reminded Smith that he should have gotten in touch with the Legion of Decency before printing his remarks. Keller told him that he had checked with a staff member of *Time*, who called the review "way off base" and said that the reviewer wrote into his comment sexual allusions that were not in the picture. Keller urged Smith to publish another editorial giving the other side of the story.

Television was the only medium that had literally grown up with the Christophers. After the single award to "Amahl" in 1951, the list grew to four the following year, three of which were Christmas specials. Over the years, Christmas and Easter programs, with their religious significance, received a goodly number of citations.

But the awards ranged widely from an occasional sitcom ("I Love Lucy," 1958) to Maurice Evans' production of *Hamlet* (1953). Documentaries received attention, as did such classics as *Great Expectations* (1954), *Peter Pan* (1955), *The Prince and the Pauper* (1957), *The Bridge of San Luis Rey* (1958), and "Mark Twain's America" (1960).

Television dramas did not figure heavily, but one exception was "Little Moon of Alban" (1958). The musical programs of Perry Como, Dinah Shore, Lawrence Welk, and variety shows such as those of Ed Sullivan and Garry Moore came in for their share of awards. Poulenc's opera, *Dialogues of the Carmelites*, was honored in 1957, along with ten other presentations. The awards were as eclectic and wide-ranging as the medium itself.

Perhaps the spirit of the once-infant medium was best caught by Lee Cooley, producer of the Perry Como Show. In a 1956 letter, he said:

> At the first television broadcasters' meeting here in New York in 1943, I was asked, as a pioneer television producer, to say something to the assembled members that might help shape the infant medium's destiny in the years to come. In effect, the little speech cautioned against lowering its moral standards in an effort to reach for sorely needed commercial dollars. The message was a gentle admonition to all of the production people present to set standards so high as to be above reproach in the sanctity of the American home. . . . I have put down the foregoing for one purpose, Father Keller, and that is to indicate to you, if possible, how deeply grateful I am to the Christophers for this particular honor. You describe it as a little "pat on the back." In my case, the pat went clear to my soul and left there a glowing hope that perhaps, in some small way, I have been able to make a tiny part of my bright dream for television come true.

Bob Banner, a three-time award-winner, picked up this theme in a 1959 letter: "You have no idea how much your 'pats on the back' are worth to those of us in the industry." And it was echoed by Arnold Peyser, a writer for the Dinah Shore Chevy Show, when he said: "You should know how important the little 'pat on the back' is when you are trying hard to keep standards in a maze of mediocrity."

Awards were given for radio programs, magazine pieces, newspaper articles, cartoons, an occasional letter to the editor, and musical compositions.

The story behind one song award deserves repeating. It concerns the mother of a GI killed in Korea in 1953. The mother wrote to the Jane Froman show, "U.S.A. Canteen," saying that she had nothing to show for her son's death except a piece of paper from the War Department. She asked: "Couldn't someone write something that would reaffirm the faith that gives the only real meaning to life?" The letter impressed Irving Mansfield, the program producer-director, who saw in this woman's petition the basis for a song. He turned it over to four songwriters—Ervin Drake, Irvin Graham, Jimmy Shirl, and Al Stillman. They came up with the words and music for "I Believe:"

> *I believe for every drop of rain that falls,*
> *a flower grows.*
> *I believe that somewhere in the darkest night,*
> *a candle glows.*
> *I believe for everyone who goes astray,*
> *someone will come to show the way.*
> *I believe, I believe.*
>
> *I believe above the storm*
> *the smallest prayer will still be heard.*
> *I believe that Someone in the great somewhere*
> *hears every word.*
> *Everytime I hear a newborn baby cry,*
> *or touch a leaf, or see the sky,*
> *Then I know why I believe.*

Keller was so moved by this story that he wanted to give the woman a word of consolation, but her letter had been misplaced among the thousands sent to CBS. So he did the next best thing. He gave the songwriters a Christopher award, commenting:

> One bereaved mother reaching out of her little world has made the bigger world better because she took the trouble to write one letter. She has reached millions with a reminder of that faith in God that gives meaning to life.

That, in a nutshell, is the purpose of the Christopher Awards.

•14•

In and Out of Hollywood

"I can still hear that marvelous laugh of his. It would burst out of him like a rocket shooting up for the sky. That was one of the things that made it so pleasant to be around him."
                                                                Loretta Young

Hollywood was familiar territory to Keller by the 1940s. He had become accustomed to turning up unannounced, from the 1920s on, at the Beverly Hills home of Gladys Belzer, whose three daughters were actresses. One of them, Loretta Young, became a staunch supporter of Maryknoll missions.

It was Loretta Young and her husband, Tom Lewis, who offered Keller their hospitality in the summer of 1946, when he desperately needed time off. Now at the mid-point of his career, he would soon be taking part in the Maryknoll Chapter that would decide the fate of the Christopher movement. For two months Keller relaxed, talked of his plans with his sympathetic friends, said Mass daily in their home, and made the most of their swimming pool. It was one of those rare periods when people could get to know him.

Loretta Young recalled that summer:

> His mind was too active for him to sit there and hibernate. He started talking about an idea he had for a book—I think it was *You Can Change the World.* My husband, Father Keller and I would sit around talking. . . . He had a gracious attitude and kindness toward everybody. I could never even get him to say that the Christopher movement was started to counteract the Communist movement here. He would say, "No, we're not

anti-anything. We're pro-Christ. . . ." His influence on me was enormous. It was coated with such human understanding of people that I never realized that it was so spiritual. He didn't talk "holier than thou. . . ." I'm convinced that the Loretta Young television shows were based on those talks we had. I didn't realize it at the time.[1]

Another member of the film community who had his observation to make was Keller's friend Ray Bolger, the dancer and entertainer, who spoke of him as "an intelligent and intense man [who] could not survive the hours of work without a sense of humor. That was his hidden asset. A sense of humor is when, at the most discouraging moment of your life, you can look at it and say 'Well, I can laugh it off.' You take a thing that's almost impossible and see it as a challenge. . . . A sense of humor is an attitude about adversity."[2]

Over the Christmas holidays in 1948, Keller gave two retreats in Hollywood—one for women (including Loretta Young, Rosalind Russell, Joan Leslie, Jeanne Crain, Georgiana Young, and Dolores Hope) and the other for men (including Fred Brisson, Tom Lewis, Paul Brinkman, Dr. Francis Griffin, and Ricardo Montalban). These individuals formed the nucleus of what film critic William Mooring called the "Hollywood Christophers." They were concerned about Communist influence in the Hollywood unions and deeply worried by what they considered the growing laxity in moral standards— meaning sex and violence. On Christmas Eve, Keller was the guest of honor at a dinner given by actress Irene Dunne (Mrs. Francis Griffin). Also present were the Lewises, Bing Crosby's brother Larry, and producers William Perlberg and Howard Emmet Rogers.

Perlberg and his partner, director George Seaton, were no strangers to Keller. Not only was the priest a frequent visitor at the Seaton home, but a few years earlier Keller had encouraged them, in the course of a round of golf, to go ahead with a film they were planning— *Miracle on Thirty-Fourth Street*. Just recently he had informally collaborated with them on *Apartment for Peggy*, which Bosley Crowther of the *New York Times* called "an enriching picture balanced with laughter and tears." The film, based on a story by Faith Baldwin, told the story of a teacher and his influence on the lives of his students, and was a tribute to Seaton's dead brother, who had been a college professor.

At this time, Keller was in the midst of his $40,000 book and drama award contest and was regarded in Hollywood as a man who meant business. Hernando Courtwright, president of the Beverly Hills Hotel, became one of his friends and introduced him to many people. Another friend was Charles Skouras, brother of producer Spyros Skouras. As president of the Fox West Coast Theaters, Charles Skouras invited Keller to address 250 theater managers in the Ambassador Hotel.

Keller remained active for years in Hollywood in a behind-the-scenes role. He encouraged Ward Bond and other members of the Screen Actors' Guild in their ultimately successful efforts to oust the Communists from their union. (He was not, however, a party to the infamous blacklisting that banned reputed Communists from writing and directing for Hollywood films.) Despite his support of conservative causes, Keller's influence was not restricted to the right wing. Dore Shary, who directed Loretta Young in *The Farmer's Daughter*, became an admirer, if not a follower, of Keller. At the Lewises' one evening, this advocate of many liberal causes declared to Keller: "I would do anything to promote the brotherhood of man." When Keller replied that a human brotherhood was not possible without a divine fatherhood, Shary became thoughtful. He could not bring himself to agree on the existence of a God, but he did not reject the possibility either.

As a missioner, Keller might have made himself at home with peasants in a Chinese rice paddy or Indians in a Bolivian jungle village. As it turned out, his mission assignment took him among the influential in America. Since golf was their favorite sport, Keller spent a lot of time on the links. Frequently, he teed off with Spyros Skouras, head of Twentieth Century–Fox, in persistent efforts to get a "Christopher slant" into his host's movies. It was something any red-blooded Communist would do, he felt, and Keller didn't mind playing by those rules.

In the spring of 1949, Keller was golfing with Bob McMahon, a lawyer for Warner Brothers. As the discussion turned inevitably to things Christopher, McMahon said to Keller: "You'll never be able to catch up with the requests for talks if you just keep on the way you're going."

Keller looked at him in puzzlement.

McMahon explained, "You couldn't catch up if you gave five

talks a day. Why don't you put the idea into a movie? That way, you could give 500 talks a day." This chance advice revolutionized Keller's life.

Never one to pass up an opportunity, he took himself off to Leo McCarey, whose Academy Award as director of *Going My Way* had made him one of Hollywood's leading lights. McCarey was sympathetic but blunt. All Keller needed, he said, was a script, a cast, a lot of money, and enough entertainment value to hold an audience. If Keller could come up with those four items, McCarey would agree to direct the film.

Keller returned to New York to pull together material for the movie from his book, *You Can Change the World*. Meanwhile, McCarey recruited Dick Breen and Eugene Ling, two respected writers, to work on the script. Keller raised $25,000 on the strength of his vision and persuasiveness. Now all he needed was an all-star cast. Loretta Young recalled how he went about assembling it:

> [Keller] called me up and said he wanted to make a little movie explaining the Christophers. He had also asked Irene Dunne, Jack Benny, Bob Hope, Bill Holden, Paul Douglas, Ann Blyth and others. They were stars in those days. . . . And so I said, "I guess so, Father."

It was decided to follow the book title and call the film, *You Can Change the World*. Producer Hal Roach lent his studio to the Christophers for the shooting. Bernard Carr of Cascade Films handled the production details. William Perlberg was the producer.

"Going to the studio that day, I made up and got dressed at home," said Young. "And Irene did the same thing. We were there ready to go like two dressed extras—and we didn't know what we were going to say."

What helped the cast was the high regard in which everyone held McCarey. On the day of filming, he worked patiently with each actor. "Anyway," said Young, "we were all professionals. The whole thing took one day."

The setting for the film, *You Can Change the World*, was Jack Benny's living room, to which the Hollywood personalities had been invited to hear a talk by Keller. Amid the chatter and by-play—some of it improvised—Keller told his listeners about the references to God in the Declaration of Independence and related some stories from his book. Bob Hope got into the act with a cameo appearance, filmed later, and Jack Benny read from Lincoln's so-called "lost speech," in which the President praised the Declaration. Bing Crosby strolled by, singing "Early American," a song written for the occasion by Jimmy Van Heusen and Johnny Burke. There were the usual cracks about Benny's stinginess and a few laughs as Paul Douglas flaunted his knowledge of history.

America's greatness—so went the underlying theme—was the result of democracy and godliness; if the country lost its religious heritage, it would collapse as every nation before it had done. The message of the film was pure Americanism, in the spirit of Archbishop Hughes or Orestes Brownson.

Was religion using nationalism, or was it the other way round? Was Keller using Hollywood, or vice versa? Keller himself saw no contradictions between these various elements and had no desire to be theoretical about them. In his hands, they were harmonious, and he had the balance not to go too far by engaging in politics.

You Can Change the World, released in 1950, was a huge success and was shown to audiences all over the country. In a ten-year period, 3,000 prints were distributed. A woman in Florida showed her copy 110 times. A man in Indiana booked 50 screenings. *You Can Change the World*, sentimental and naïve by the standards of the sixties, appealed to the majority of Americans in the fifties. As an indication of its acceptability to those in government, the film was shown to personnel at the U.S. State Department.

Buoyed by his success in Hollywood, Keller returned to New York by way of Washington, where he met twice with members of the Atomic Energy Commission. The way had been prepared for him by Thomas E. Murray, a member of the body and an old friend from Southampton days.[3] Murray was a strong believer in the peacetime uses of the atom, and persuaded Keller to make a popular film on the subject. Called *Atomic Energy Can Be a Blessing*, the second Christopher film was made in New York in 1950. Like most Americans, Keller could not believe that the government would ever expose its soldiers and civilians to atomic radiation, as recent evidence has proven to be the case in tests in Nevada from 1953–1962. More than ten years later, Keller clung to this optimistic view of atomic energy, when he invited as his TV guest Dr. Edward

Teller, a nuclear cold-warrior, the so-called "father of the H-Bomb."

During 1950 Keller followed up the first two films with *Television Is What You Make It* and *Government Is Your Business*, though the latter remained uncompleted for some time. These dramatic films were expensive—each cost at least $30,000—and Keller was constrained in his fund-raising efforts by Maryknoll's stipulation that he had to have money in the bank before he could begin production. His original aim—to make these films a teaching aid for his network of career guidance schools—had been thwarted by the demise of this plan, so he turned to the nation's television stations, which were just beginning their phenomenal growth. In 1952, Keller sent letters to all 120 stations then in existence. To his surprise, 48 of them agreed to schedule the Christopher films free of charge. The government film was accepted by the National Broadcasting Company for viewing on the eve of the Republican National Convention in July 1952—a prime-time opportunity. Had he been willing to forgo this chance to reach a nationwide audience of perhaps seven million, Keller had the assurance of Spyros Skouras that it would be shown in every Fox theater in the country. Faced with the choice, Keller showed a prescience that might have been the envy of the shrewdest Hollywood producer. He threw in his lot with television. It was a decision the studios would eventually be forced to make, as Los Angeles became the TV production capital of the world. But in the early fifties the two were as hostile as rival football leagues.

In order to make any sort of impact on the television-watching public, Keller knew he had to get into weekly programming. Producing regularly scheduled dramatic shows was out of the question; he had neither the budget nor the available talent to attempt such an undertaking. Nor would an occasional extravaganza accomplish his purpose. Instead, he devised a plan to produce weekly interview programs on which he would talk to guests who reflected the Christopher idea in thought and action. Even this was a formidable task. So he asked Hugh Rogers, an executive with Batten, Barton, Durstine and Osborn, the giant New York advertising agency, for his advice. Rogers recommended a former BBD&O filmmaker who had just started his own production company in Hollywood. His name was Jack Denove, and he proved to be a happy choice.

•15•

Television Is What You Make It

"Our Lord used weddings, dinners, parties and many types of worldly occasions as well as persons, both good and bad, to remind men of their spiritual destiny. . . . Combining informal and dignified entertainment with a Christopher message is a most effective way to emphasize individual responsibility and initiative in restoring God's order to the world."   James Keller

Jack Denove was a short, stocky, gravel-voiced native of Brooklyn who had been by turns a police reporter on New York papers, a promoter of semipro basketball games, and a top director of films made by BBD&O.

In certain respects, Denove and Keller became very close. They both had a dedication—almost an addiction—to work; each had a sense of humor; and Denove understood the peculiar amalgam of religious and patriotic values that constituted the "Christopher message." Early in 1952, they made plans to produce twenty fifteen-minute films for television—at the rock-bottom price of $3,000 each. Denove was to produce and direct the films, and Keller agreed to line up the guests with help from "Judge" Carberry, a somewhat mysterious Hollywood figure who had access to stars Keller did not personally know.

The informal—as distinct from the dramatic—programs were filmed conversations shot with two cameras running simultaneously for thirty minutes, "almost like a newsreel," as Keller put it. The best material was edited into a quarter-hour program. Denove made the first two shows at cost, with the remainder to be done at a modest 10 or 15 percent markup. The producer-director promised that "I will put everything I've got into making the films as good as possible . . . as an opportunity to make a small contribution to the great work you are doing." He was as good as his word.

In the spring of 1952, production began for the weekly interview programs. As Denove's and Keller's expertise increased, they were able to shoot as many as eight programs a day. Technicians were paid union wages, musicians were given an honorarium, and the various stars and personalities donated their services. By the end of the year, "The Christopher Program" was appearing on about fifty television stations, frequently on Sunday afternoons or in the early evening hours. Meanwhile, new stations were opening at the rate of one a week. Keller pursued them so vigorously that by 1954, 202 stations carried his show. He had made nearly 100 programs by then, but it was a constant race for Keller, amid other work, to feed the yawning void of television programming.

Among the hundreds of "name performers" from Hollywood, Broadway, radio, and TV who came to chat with Keller in the first few years were Fred Allen, Don Ameche, Rosalind Russell, and Dinah Shore. So vital did Keller consider television programming that he sometimes cancelled an issue of Christopher News Notes to raise enough money to pay for it.

Not all of Hollywood by any means flocked to "The Christopher Program." Some stars were not interested. Others, like Lucille Ball, were not invited because of their alleged "leftist" leanings. Comedian Jerry Lewis lost his chance because of a parody he did on the Last Supper at a Las Vegas night club.

"The Christopher Program" was popular for good reasons. Because of Denove's experience, the production values were high. Stations welcomed the nondenominational approach of Keller and the fact that the program featured stars who were seldom, if ever, seen on television at that time. Also Keller consistently refused to solicit funds from viewers.

One of the best known of the interview programs was a thirty-minute program called "Faith, Hope and Hogan." Made in 1954, it was filmed in a five-hour period at Thunderbird Golf Club, near Palm Springs, California. Bob Hope and Bing Crosby agreed to appear with golfer Ben Hogan, who discussed his remarkable comeback after an automobile accident five years before that almost took his life. The program had no script, a fact that caused some consternation on Hogan's part and much amusement to veterans Hope and Crosby. As Keller described the filming:

> Our director, Jack Denove, moved three cameras and a studio crew of 25 men to a golf course in the desert near Palm Springs, 125 miles east of Los Angeles. The whole film had to be shot before the sun would disappear behind the mountains. Thanks be to God, the film turned out to be much better than anyone had expected.

Keller's only advice to Hogan was to say "whatever comes to mind." The champion golfer described no miraculous intervention. He said he returned to top form by "working a little harder than I ever had before." Crosby did his bit by singing two songs, "Accentuate the Positive" and "One Little Candle," both of which expressed the Christopher message. And Hope added his usual string of one-liners, then ended on a spiritual note by reciting the Prayer of St. Francis: "Lord, make me an instrument of Your peace. . . ."

NBC officials in Burbank, California, liked the film so much that they made it available to the network. Keller estimated that upward of twenty million people saw this mixture of sports, entertainment, and inspiration. He commented: "The people in entertainment, sports and similar fields are anxious to have the Christophers use their experiences as settings to focus attention on spiritual and patriotic ideas."

Nor were the dramatic films forgotten. Keller's original aim was to produce forty-eight of them, but later he scaled the number down to thirty-six, eventually settling for one-third that number. Denove's job was to line up and direct the scriptwriters. It was an exercise in frustration, as this letter from Denove to Keller (3/54) reveals:

> There have been times in the last several weeks in working with writers that I have wanted to call the whole thing off. You can spend hours with them developing the point. They read your books and see your present pictures and still, somehow, they can't see what we are driving at.

Finally, writer Larry Marcus produced an acceptable film treatment for "Link in a Chain," the story of a college professor who thought he had wasted his life teaching for forty years until persuaded otherwise by his students. James Cagney starred in his TV debut. The classic film "tough guy" had consistently refused his friend Robert Montgomery's entreaties that he appear on the new medium, but Keller got him to say yes just by asking. Questioned whether he planned to continue in television, Cagney replied: "Not unless Father Keller needs me again." Another dramatic program made in 1954 starred Paul Kelly as a rancher who opposed a nuclear plant until convinced of the atom's value in medicine, agriculture, and as a force for peace.

As always, the search for funding went on. Keller was particularly successful with H. Roy Cullen, a Houston oilman. After about eighteen months of correspondence, Keller obtained $25,000 from the Texan for the second atomic energy film. Along with his check, Cullen wrote:

> You should have been a businessman for, with your salesmanship ability, you would have no trouble selling gold bricks. You have sold me again, and I am going to finance your number two item, "Atomic Energy as a Force for Good." I will give you $25,000 and let you try that one out.

Cullen was so pleased with the film that he arranged a special showing for the governor of Texas, the mayor of Houston, and a number of university officials.

Another contribution—$25,000 for a program on juvenile delinquency—came from the Fisher Foundation in Detroit. It was called "The World Starts with Jimmy," and starred William Campbell and Dorothy Malone.

Knowing that Denove was working on a limited cash margin, Keller tried to keep his checks coming as soon as he had the money. Ann Denove, Jack's wife, recalled: "While we didn't make a lot of profit, there was a film strike around that time and the Christopher account kept us in business." On one occasion a Christopher check arrived unsigned. Denove responded:

> The Angels came bearing a much-desired check. But when we started to cash it, we were told it was very lovely but it still

needed the Chief Angel's signature—so I am sending it back. I do hope you can return it to us as soon as you get it.

By the summer of 1954, the quarter-hour programs were replaced by informal half-hours. The length of programs varied from year to year as market conditions changed. During late 1954 and early 1955, the Christopher program was made in New York, while Jack Denove occupied himself with the production and subsequent problems connected with an hour-long show sponsored by the Bank of America.

The informal programs revolved around such topics as family values, love of country, the importance of voting and jury duty, and examples from many career fields of what "one person can do." Sometimes performers were asked to read from the words of Washington, Jefferson, Lincoln, John Adams, Daniel Webster, or the signers of the Declaration of Independence. The programs wedded the heroes of the past, who believed in God and the democratic experiment, to the heroes of the present, who contributed their time and talents to the cause of a priest who was hard to turn down. The programs did not emphasize distinctively Catholic beliefs, but stressed God and the Ten Commandments. Keller's black suit and Roman collar identified him, and that was enough.

As the programs went on, guests from various public-interest fields reaffirmed the values of general participation in current affairs. The appeal of the programs was not that Keller did them so well (he was conscious of many shortcomings) but that nobody else on television was delivering that kind of message to a mass audience. Always, Keller came back to what "you" can do. At the end of each show, he would turn directly to the camera and expound on a brief passage from the Bible. Many considered this the most effective portion of the program. Keller's sincerity was unmistakable and often compelling.

Keller traveled to Florida late in 1954 and came back with new friends and a wealth of historical information on George Washington, which he had obtained from a woman who had spent her life collecting documents on the first President. It provided the basis for several programs of readings from Washington's written works, one of which was narrated by Fred Allen, John Daly, Ella Raines, and Thelma Ritter. These programs proved to be popular, and material from them was made into a Christopher booklet, "George Washington Speaks for Himself."

In 1955, Keller did five shows with readings from the works of General Robert E. Lee, which proved popular with Southern audiences. The same year, he interviewed former President Herbert Hoover, who talked about his work on the reorganization of government. "He was inspiring," Keller noted, "and is responsible for one of the best informal movies we have in the series."

After completing these programs in New York, Keller hopped a plane west to work on the completion of five dramatic shows. Denove had cleared the decks, secured acceptable scripts, and was ready for the shooting. "Damien"—a dramatization of Father Damien's life among the lepers of Molokai, starring Stephen McNally and Victor Jory—was followed by "Sentence Deferred"—the story of John Augustus, a New England bootmaker whose efforts led to the court probation system, with Edgar Buchanan. Then came "The Two Worlds of Ann Foster"—a drama about a successful designer who had "everything money could buy," except happiness, with an introduction by Barbara Stanwyck and starring Virginia Grey. "Knock on Every Door"—about a lonely widow who became involved in political precinct work, with Gladys Hurlbut, Richard Erdman, and Toni Gerry—was the fourth dramatic show. "Decision for Life"—the early adventures of Florence Nightingale, played by Cathy O'Donnell—was the final program produced at this time. The filming of these five was completed during two weeks in October and three in November.

Other Christopher dramatic programs told the story of one man's struggle against union corruption; and a woman's lifelong efforts to promote humane treatment of the mentally ill (Dorothea Dix).

During this period of intense activity, two informal half-hour programs were also completed. In addition, one weekend, Keller traveled to San Francisco to attend a dinner at the Mark Hopkins Hotel for a large number of Christopher friends. He also played host at a dinner at the Bel Air Hotel in Los Angeles for 170 Hollywood personalities and supporters who had helped make the Christopher programs possible.

Back in New York just before Christmas 1955, Keller interviewed Rose Kennedy, wife of the former Ambassador to Great Britain. A month later, John F. Kennedy, now a senator, was a guest on the Christophers, where he talked about his book, *Profiles in Courage*. A voracious reader and no more inclined to "waste time" than Keller himself, the youthful senator kept his nose buried in a book while waiting for the show to begin. He all but ignored his sister Jean, who was working for the Christophers at that time. In 1956, Robert F. Kennedy, who was looking into corruption in the labor-management field, made a Christopher program in which he stressed the importance of getting young people into government. Dr. Tom Dooley, who was something of a legend for his medical work among refugees in Southeast Asia, was also a Christopher guest during this period.

It was back and forth from coast to coast for Keller and Denove for the rest of the 1950s. One series of five shows was done in the nation's capital in March 1956. Bob Considine, who suggested the idea, introduced the programs, which included as guests experts from the Atomic Energy Commission, the State Department, the Postal Service, the Library of Congress, and the National Gallery of Art. Another series was a group of thirteen biblical dramatizations edited from footage Keller had purchased from a filmmaker in Rome, which were narrated for Christopher showings by Sir Cedric Hardwicke.

In an issue of Christopher News Notes for May 1957, there was a listing of 94 guests and 42 personalities from the world of film, television, and Broadway who had taken part in 52 programs over the previous year.

Robert Young recalled an incident that occurred during this time in California:

> Father Keller came by our house in Beverly Hills to deliver a script for me to read on the Christopher program. He was wearing khaki pants and a rumpled shirt. My wife looked out the window and thought he was a gardener applying for a job. "Go around to the back," she told him. He dutifully did so and explained to the cook the reason for his visit. When she learned who it was, my wife Betty fell all over him.

By 1955, the number of television stations carrying the Christophers rose above the 300 mark and stayed there for about five years. In a letter to Bishop Lane of Maryknoll, Keller wrote:

All goes well at this end, thanks to so many blessings—especially in TV and radio. Even though most of our programs are not too hot, due to low budget and necessary haste in making them, the stations gobble them up. We are now on 310 TV stations and 920 radio each week—at an average of only 10,000 listeners a station, this would mean 12 million reached weekly.

Keller's figures, like those of most independent producers, must be examined with care, but his audience was a sizable one.

In the same letter, Keller mentioned that the DuPont Company was so impressed by the dramatic shows that their executives asked their advertising agency—none other than BBD&O—why the Christophers were making better pictures than they were. This must have pleased Jack Denove when he heard about it.

A candid assessment of some of the "brainstorming" sessions—conducted by a wide range of Keller's friends and acquaintances—was contained in this letter to Lane (3/1/58):

In order to preserve spontaneity, we have no rehearsals and do not present the subject for discussion until participants reach the studio. It is amazing to see the practical suggestions which the average individual will give. . . . The answers and reactions of the various participants are not earth-shaking, to be sure. In fact, a few even "freeze up" and we will no doubt have to discard some film, edit, or throw it away. But the majority make comments that are most worthwhile and sensible and reflect sound spiritual values.

In 1957, Keller launched a series of "Christopher Thoughts for Today"—one-minute radio spots. These were placed on 230 stations at the beginning, but before long were being heard daily on more than 2,000 stations. The spots were based on stories that appeared in the newspaper column, which in turn were collected in the annual "three-minutes-a-day" book. Once a good "Christopher" story was found, it was sure to be used in a variety of ways.

Critics of Christopher television and radio programs often took Keller to task for the blandness of the presentations. The shows avoided controversial topics, such as the race issue, the morality of a nuclear deterrent, religious tensions among Catholics, Protestants, and Jews, and thorny moral issues such as divorce, birth control, and abortion. Instead they frequently focused on "motherhood and apple pie" matters. Keller knew his limitations and steered clear of sensitive areas. He stayed on safe ground, but it was almost virgin territory: by pointing out what one person can do, he offended almost no one but stirred the dormant energies of many. Few, if any, preachers of his day talked to the individual in such challenging, but reassuring, terms. If there was a religious void in the fifties, Keller did his best—inadequate though it might have been—to fill it. He loved to quote Cardinal Newman: "Nothing would be done at all if a man waited till he could do it so well that no one could find fault with it."

Whatever their shortcomings, Christopher programs generated much positive listener reaction. A Jewish businessman in Lansing, Michigan, wrote Keller to say that he had been on the point of refusing to become chairman of an important charity drive. "If I hadn't been listening to the television program," he said, "I would have turned it down. But after watching that program each week, I would have been ashamed to say 'No.' "

A teacher in Wisconsin made this comment: "Saw your TV program last night. I was about to resign my job next Friday. After hearing the Christopher message, I have changed my mind." A state lawmaker put it this way: "These programs have been a source of courage and guidance to me in my everyday task here in the Nebraska Legislature."

But perhaps the most lasting effect on television of the Christopher idea was made by a woman who used the medium to bring reading and math skills to nine million American youngsters each week and children in more than fifty countries. Joan Ganz Cooney, creator of the "Sesame Street" series, gave much of the credit to Keller:

> My involvement in television is a commercial for the Christopher movement. When I was a teenager, I first started reading Father Keller, and he had a profound influence on my life. He said that unless idealists take jobs in the media—radio, newspapers, television—people without ideals may take those jobs. I started as a reporter, and then went into television. I came to New York and went to work for NBC, and publicized television shows for several years. When Channel 13, the educational

channel in New York, opened in 1959, I was there when the doors opened![1]

In 1966, Cooney, then a producer at Channel 13, was asked by the Carnegie Foundation to investigate the possibilities of using television in preschool education. With funding from the Carnegie and Ford Foundations and the U.S. Office of Education, the Children's Television Workshop was formed in 1968 with Joan Ganz Cooney as executive director.

"But Father Keller," she added, "was the cause of it all." Cooney's public acknowledgment of the Christopher influence on her career is a tribute to the force of an idea. As much as anyone in his time, Keller popularized the concept of public service. Most of those who heard his message and acted on it remain unknown and unacknowledged outside their own sphere. There is no way of measuring the cumulative effect of Keller's repeated exhortations to "light a candle," but it cannot be small.

Tom Lewis, a radio and television producer himself (who had had ample opportunity to observe Keller during his two-month visit in 1946), made this assessment of the man:

> Keller was gentle. He was persistent. He knew what he was doing. Maybe he had to do it in a self-deprecating way because he didn't have public presence. He was not a fireball. He was not the prophet Jeremiah. His quiet approach was most effective. I honestly believe that everyone he ever talked to, whether they completely understood it or not, was affected by him.

·16·

Government Is Your Business

"It has become habitual and perhaps fashionable to disdain government as something beneath us. Today the chief obstacle to good government is the widespread belief that it is a job for someone else, not for us."   James Keller

Keller was a prodigious worker in the office or out of it. The beaches and resorts of the Atlantic coast—Maine, Cape Cod, Newport, Southampton, the Jersey shore—provided the setting for his persuasive powers no less than did midtown Manhattan. At any of these watering spots, unsuspecting vacationers would seek to escape the world for a respite only to encounter this cheerful priest who reminded them it was their duty to change it. In some cases, Keller's insistence on "what one person can do" was applied for many years.

One example of Keller's ability to change a life was that of Gerard C. Smith, whose relationship with the priest went back a long way. Smith recalled:

> It was about 1931 when [Keller] came to visit the Murrays. I think we must have seen him at dinner and on the beach. He would swim and lie in the sun. He was an extraordinarily handsome fellow, one of the greatest enthusiasts I ever ran across. He was infectious; he'd talk to a bunch of youngsters and have them spellbound.[1]

One thing in particular impressed Smith about Keller:

> He had this obsession with work, more so than any man I know, perhaps with the exception of Jean Monnet, who was the foun-

150

der of [modern] Europe. With Monnet, the conversation always turned to European problems. Same thing with Keller. He never wasted any time with small talk. . . . He certainly made an impact on me. More than anything else, my contact with him led me to believe that I oughtn't just practice law, but try to do something in the government. I came down [to Washington] in 1950, just after the Korean War had started. And I think that the constant hammering that "you can change the world" had something to do with it.

Gerard Smith worked in Washington as assistant to Thomas E. Murray, a member of the Atomic Energy Commission, until 1954, when he transferred to the State Department as special assistant to Secretary of State John Foster Dulles for atomic energy affairs. Later he was Assistant Secretary in charge of the Policy Planning Staff for Dulles and his successor, Christian Herter. After that, Smith returned to private law practice and started a magazine called *Interplay*, which sought to strengthen American ties with Western Europe. In 1969, he was recalled to government and became the head of the Nixon administration's Arms Control Agency. He is credited with being the force behind the first (and only) Strategic Arms Limitation Treaty (SALT). Under President Carter, Smith was appointed Special Representative for [nuclear] Nonproliferation Matters. In the spring of 1982, Smith joined Robert McNamara, McGeorge Bundy, and George F. Kennan in proposing that NATO renounce its policy that permits the first use of nuclear weapons. Although Smith and Keller were not in complete harmony on their political philosophies, Smith commented:

I felt that Father Keller ideologically was very conservative in terms of his general political-economic approach. I think he felt that I wasn't this conservative but he never let that show at all. I never had any feeling that he was argumentative.

Smith had this to say about Keller's spirituality:

The characteristic that pops up in my mind about Keller is that, while there are lots of worldly priests—and, in a sense, he was a worldly priest—he kept his spirituality and his intense interest in non-worldly things better than any worldly priest I have ever met. And while he seemed to enjoy being surrounded by the "beautiful people" in Southampton, the sun and the sea, he was constantly working on how he could change the world.

Another Keller "convert" to public service was Thomas Pike, who had made his mark in the oil drilling business in California and, in the process, had become an alcoholic. Shortly before he met Keller, Pike had joined Alcoholics Anonymous and was looking for a constructive way to spend his free time. As Pike related in his privately published *Memoirs:*

> In the Fall of 1946 Katherine and I met . . . Father James Keller at the home of Bob and Dolores Hope. . . . I was deeply moved by this dynamic priest and the exciting potential of his powerful idea with its central themes—"You can change the world" and "It is better to light one candle than to curse the darkness. . . ." It actually changed the course of my whole life.

Pike's first foray into the marketplace as a Christopher was to initiate a profit-sharing plan for the employees of the Pike Drilling Company:

> Our competitors accused us, of everything from foul play and unfair competition to socialism and communism. Nevertheless, because it was based on sound fundamentals of incentive, recognition, participation and extra reward for extra productivity, it worked well for us and paid off handsomely for all concerned . . . workers, managers and owners.

As Pike looked around for "other worlds to conquer," with his newfound sobriety and energy, he thought of Keller's words: "It's a question of getting the good people into action on the firing line of life in politics and government." He involved himself in California politics, attended the Republican National Convention in 1948, and backed Richard Nixon's bid for the Senate in 1950. After the Eisenhower victory in 1952, he was called to Washington to serve in the Pentagon as deputy to Charles A. Thomas, the Assistant Secretary of Defense for Supply and Logistics. It was a frustrating and rewarding experience. In 1954, he himself became Assistant Secretary. Of Keller's influence on him, Pike said:

He was a realist . . . and it occurred to him that even men who were selfishly pursuing careers in business and making a lot of money could have an effect on improving this old world if they'd realize what they could do. Jim had the really extraordinary vision of seeing what ordinary people—if there is such a thing— could do about improving the situation and changing the world.[2]

Some years later, in an effort to encourage young people to prepare themselves for "Christopher careers," Thomas Pike established an endowment for a Christopher Scholarship at Loyola-Marymount University in Los Angeles:

They started the custom last year of having Katherine and me out to lunch to meet the Christopher Scholars. They are the nicest, finest, strongest-looking bunch of kids you ever saw.

Another public servant influenced by Keller was Richard Kneip, who had been introduced to Keller's writings by his pastor in South Dakota.[3] In a letter to the author (5/18/81) Kneip wrote:

I was profoundly touched by Father Keller and the inspirational writings, zeal and enthusiasm of this one man. . . . I doubt seriously if I have ever given a speech . . . that did not include a direct or indirect reference to his writings and attitudes. . . . In his book, *You Can Change the World*, are perfect examples of simple, basic thoughts that people need to be reminded of constantly and, if followed, can change the course of this entire world. In my case, his words became the forerunner and inspiration for my personal involvement in the business community, the State Senate, Governorships, American Ambassador to the Republic of Singapore, and even now as I embark on a new business career. . . . I reveal with great fondness my appreciation of Father Keller, my introduction to his words by Bishop Anderson, and the profound impact it has had on my life.

* * *

In 1950 Fulton and Grace Oursler invited Keller to visit them on Cape Cod. It was there on the beach that Keller got the idea for a book that would encourage the average citizen to become involved in government. As he told the Ourslers about the finishing touches he was putting on his volume, *Careers That Change Your World*, Mrs. Oursler turned to him and said: "Why don't you write a book on good government?" The idea took root, and the result was *Government Is Your Business*, a book written for "the man in the street, the housewife in the home." In the foreword, Keller put it this way:

> Primarily, this book was written to remind each citizen of his own personal, individual responsibility toward his government. All government receives its authority from God through the people, or, as Jefferson put it, "through the consent of the governed." Therefore, the responsibility of government resides first in the citizen: it comes from him and it should be directed toward him. It is his job to see that it does. . . . Coupled with an abiding faith in the goodness of God, these ideas have proved down through the ages that they belong in the formula for successful living.

A listing of the chapter headings tells what the book is about, as well as the spirit in which it was written:

1. It's Your Country Too!
2. Everyone Can Do Something
3. Politics Affects You Whether You Realize It or Not
4. The Beginnings of Government
5. City Government Depends on You
6. State Government Vitally Affects You
7. It's Your National Government
8. What Everybody Should Know about Civil Service
9. The Source of American Strength

Each chapter contained four subchapters, and an appendix reproduced the Declaration of Independence and the Constitution of the United States of America, with its Bill of Rights and other amendments. Published by Doubleday in 1951, it was updated and reprinted in 1959. Leo Egan, Albany correspondent for the *New York Times*, wrote most of the book, especially the sections on city and state government. But the anecdotes and the facility for turning negative situations into opportunities were vintage Keller.

One of the experts asked to make comments before publication was Father George Higgins of the Social Action Department of the National Catholic Welfare Conference. Higgins found little to criticize, other than Keller's repeated allusions to high taxes. He also thought that the anti-Communist rhetoric, especially as it applied to members of the State Department, was overdone. To the section on states' rights, he recommended adding something on states' responsibilities, particularly in the area of minimum wages and racial equality. He urged Keller to put in a good word for the State Department's Point IV (foreign aid) Program. He also felt the book went overboard in its praise of the FBI. He said:

> I recognize the wonderful work being done by the FBI, but I know a number of very responsible government officials who honestly believe that there are some serious faults in the FBI and who are convinced, furthermore, that the FBI has done the greatest self-publicity job in the world. I mention this consideration merely to suggest the dangers of giving all-out approval to the FBI. Not all the critics of the FBI, by any means, are pro-communist.

But Higgins was pleased with the book in general. He liked the emphasis on the importance of adequate salaries for government employees.

Government Is Your Business had a large sale—over 300,000 copies.

One reader who took the admonitions on the high cost of government to heart, wrote to tell Keller that he had just started his government job, after going to college at night. His family savings had dropped from $800 to about $150. Nevertheless, he said:

> Has it been worth it? . . . I think the answer is *yes*. To begin with, I now have my degree, with highest honors. More important, I am now serving the United States of America—the stenographers, typists, bank clerks, butchers, bakers and factory workers whose hard-earned money will be paying my salary. . . . It is enough to say that I shall certainly not be "boondoggling." Our organization has magnificent morale and a genuine belief in personal initiative. I fully intend to earn every single nickel that all those hard-pressed, heavily taxed fellow-citizens of mine are paying me.

A woman in Brooklyn ordered additional copies of the book for distribution to her Independent Citizens' Club in East New York. She wrote on September 9, 1952, that she knew "how hard it is to convince the youth of today to become interested in the community and the government as a whole. . . . While reading it . . . I'm glad that I was not wrong saying what I did to these young men and women."

Charles Perlitz, a Houston oilman, counseled a young man who had been inspired by the book to run for Railroad Commissioner, an important post in Texas politics.

The Secretary of State of Minnesota asked for a copy of the book because "I am called upon to do a great deal of public speaking and have used on many occasions thoughts and ideas and statements taken from the Christopher (News) Notes."

J. Walter Kennedy wrote to tell Keller that he had just been elected mayor of the city of Stamford, Connecticut (11/18/59). "It was the biggest landslide in the city's history," he wrote. "As I told you during our short visit in Stamford last spring, I was motivated to make this first political run by my admiration and respect for the Christopher's movement."

Another testimony to the effect of the Christopher idea on government showed the enduring nature of the printed word. A legislator in the Massachusetts House of Representatives wrote in 1966 that his sister had given him a copy of *Government Is Your Business*. As he put it:

> I firmly believe it changed my life. It gave me the insight that the road of the "individual" working to do good is not an easy road, and the examples in the book gave me the moral support and confidence to hold my ground when the going got rough.
>
> Because your book has affected my life so much, I have set as one of my goals in life to give your book to as many people as I can who I feel have the desire to change the world for the better. To date, I have given out some sixty books.

Typical of the many favorable reviews was this one, printed in the March 1952 issue of *Management Review*, a business publication, and written by Andrew J. Hayes, Contract Administrator, Texas Instruments, Inc.:

How desirable it would be for America if these persons would invest a small portion of their time in reading a book which points out how the need for higher standards of morality in government may be filled, strives to reconcile and minimize prejudices, and which offers hope. . . .

Over the years, Keller wrote to public figures on matters he thought transcended partisan politics. In the late 1940s, he sent messages to President Truman and Secretary of State Dean Acheson, urging them to oppose the admission of Red China into the United Nations. In 1956, he sent this letter to Dwight Eisenhower, who was about to begin his second term as President:

These are busy days for you, we know. And yet it occurred to me that you might find it of interest to know something about what is commonly referred to as "George Washington's Prayer."

On June 8, 1783, at his Newburgh headquarters, on the occasion of the disbanding of the army, George Washington composed a circular letter, which was to be sent to the governors of all the then-existing states. He asked the governors to bring it to the attention of their legislatures. In the closing paragraph of this letter, he implored the Divine benediction upon the country.

Keller then quoted the text of Washington's prayer, and concluded:

We have all been extremely impressed by many of your statements containing reference to God and to spiritual values. My thought was that this inspiring action and prayer of our first President might be of value to you in formulating plans on your Inauguration Day, especially since you are taking your Oath of Office on Washington's Bible.

Eisenhower never used Washington's prayer, but one adaptation of a Christopher idea found its way into the inaugural address of his successor. During the campaign of 1960, a Christopher News Note called "VOTE Intelligently, VOTE Conscientiously, VOTE Patriotically" was sent to the Christopher mailing list of more than one million. Republican and Democratic committees seized on it and orders for hundreds of thousands came pouring into Christopher headquarters. One of the points, under the heading "Tips for a Good Citizen," read as follows:

> Remind your friends to think more of what they owe their country, and less of what it owes them.

On January 20, 1961, President John F. Kennedy, in his inaugural address, said:

> Ask not what America will do for you, but what together we can do for the freedom of man.

In the early 1960s, when Richard Nixon was out of office and working for a law firm in New York, a small dinner was given for him. Keller was among the fifteen or twenty guests who attended. Nixon told the dinner guests that, when he entered Congress on his first day in the 1940s, another freshman congressman approached him and gave him a copy of the book, *You Can Change the World*, saying that he might enjoy it. The other freshman was John F. Kennedy. Keller's book was one of the few things the two men had in common.

Keller was in a Cleveland department store autographing his just-published autobiography on the day Kennedy was assassinated. Shortly afterwards, he received the following letter from a woman who had been in the store with him that day:

> I am a great admirer of yours and of what you are doing. I just got a thought to write you and let you know I have just watched your program on television with Robert Young. I can still see the tear that fell down your cheek when you were here in Cleveland when President Kennedy was murdered. . . .

Keller's ideas on government were uncomplicated, some would say simplistic. Yet his book, *Government Is Your Business*, was a detailed and accurate handbook for anyone who wanted to get more deeply involved in the political process. Moreover, it was inspiring in the basic sense that it aroused a spirit of service that did not indulge in negativism or petty politicking. From the letters that reached Christopher headquarters in the 1950s, 1960s, and even 1970s, it can safely be assumed that literally thousands of people took to heart Keller's dictum that "government is your business."

•*17*•

Critics Left and Right

> *"I'm sure you don't want to do any harm, but in spreading even one point about the Christophers that is not true, you would be giving great comfort to the Devil. These are times especially when we should be drawing together and not dividing."*
> James Keller

James Keller frequently expressed surprise that the Christopher movement was not criticized more strongly. There was, in fact, surprisingly little criticism, and that, in general, came from those who held extremist viewpoints.

One such attack from the liberal left appeared in *The Nation*, which described itself as "America's leading liberal weekly since 1865." In the issue of May 13, 1950, Carey McWilliams, a staff contributor, asked "Who Are the Christophers?"

The author did not find it easy to answer his own question:

> The Christopher movement, which might best be described as the Catholic counterpart of Moral Rearmament, is one of the more interesting of current American movements. Although "under Catholic auspices," it manages to avoid direct stress on Catholic doctrine. . . . Without a program, the Christopher movement has the same exasperating doctrinal vagueness as MRA; for example, wages must be "fair," profits must not be "excessive," and so forth.

Although the Christophers had no "program," McWilliams did attribute to the movement a definite ideology—that the one percent of "troublemakers" in the country were to be replaced by another one percent of "healthy-minded Americans." The writer tried to be fair:

> Father Keller is neither a rabble-rouser nor a demagogue; on the contrary, he is by all accounts a man of genuine good will, kindly, generous, and charitable. He is very careful, therefore, to urge his followers to show Christian love to everyone, including the Communists, and to avoid even the appearance of red-baiting.

Still, McWilliams expressed concern about the contemplated Christopher "guidance schools," as well as the Christopher influence in the motion picture industry. Although the author said there was nothing improper about "this display of zeal," as, for example, pushing for religiously oriented motion pictures, his underlying uneasiness was that "for some time now movements of the 'right' have not been balanced by movements of the 'left.' " The prospect of a Christopher effort to follow up the star-studded film, *You Can Change the World*, by a series of thirty further movies costing $1 million made the *Nation* writer uncomfortable. He quoted Justice Brandeis to the effect that "the great dangers to liberty lurk in insidious encroachments by men of zeal, well-meaning but without understanding."

McWilliams concluded his vaguely worded critique:

> These dangers become greater when people of zeal are organized into "movements" without programs or clear-cut objectives, when an ideology "given" by a leader is offered as a substitute for social goals determined by popular discussion.

A pot shot from the extreme left was published without by-line in the December 1954 *Exposé*, which called itself "a non-partisan newspaper which publishes stories and articles most papers dare not print." Its editor was Lyle Stuart. Paul Krassner was managing editor. The lead article ran under the headline: "CHRISTOPHERS WORK TO BEAT THE DEVIL." The movement was described as a "propaganda and pressure instrument that operates without formal Catholic limitations."

The *Exposé* article expressed grudging admiration for the fact that the first printing of the book *You Can Change the World* reached 55,000 copies. But it had little good to say of the book itself:

> Its effects have been felt in many fields, and always on the side of censorship, suppression and conformity.
>
> And yet the Christophers lacked all the trappings of a Catholic Action movement. They were not violent and they were not blatant. They did not sell rosaries filled with holy water and they did not (in the beginning) ask for money.

After a fairly accurate description of Christopher activities, the *Exposé* article took aim at the annual awards presentation:

> It is all part of the pattern of recruiting "good" people into films, television, newspapers and government. According to *Protestants and Other Americans United for the Separation of Church and State*, this is done "with the expectation that Roman Catholic policies may thereby come to exert a dominant influence in our society."

Exposé noted with dismay that Keller had recently called upon his followers to write their senators and congressmen in avor of adding the words "under God" to the Pledge of Allegiance.

The article concluded:

> The question in the minds of some Americans is whether the Christophers light candles or whether they light matches. And if they light matches, is our Constitution and Bill of Rights liable to be burned up in the conflagration?

All attempts by the newspaper's editors to elicit a response to the "30 questions" they wished to ask him received only Keller's genial response: "God bless you."

Keller rather liked being attacked by those who were associated in the public mind with Communists because it provided some reassurance that he was making headway. He took rather more seriously the volleys from the right and generally answered them in detail. One such letter, chiding him for "not being Catholic enough," reached him by way of McCarthy at Maryknoll. It was critical of a speech Keller had given the year before in St. Louis in which he allegedly "watered down" Catholic doctrine. In reply, Keller told his correspondent that he had asked one of his staff who had heard the lecture whether she had had the same impression. Her response was, "Not at all! As a matter of fact, I thought it was so wonderful that so many people outside of the Church were at last hearing something so Catholic."

Keller assured the letter-writer that "everything about the Christopher movement is checked and double-checked by outstanding theologians, as well as by several enthusiastic friends among the Cardinals, Archbishops and Bishops throughout the United States."

After citing instances of people returning to the sacraments or becoming Catholics as a result of Christopher influence, Keller said he had sent to Monsignor John A. Fearns, the censor of the Archdiocese of New York, for his comments the following excerpts from a speech:

> As true followers of Christ, we have a fourfold obligation:
> 1. to those who are members of the Catholic Church;
> 2. to those who are interested in entering the Church;
> 3. to those who have no desire or who refuse to become Catholics;
> 4. to those who hate the Church and fight against it.
>
> Most Catholics show a laudable interest in the first two groups. But much remains to be done in regard to the other two. . . . If we succeed in nothing more than getting them to be one degree more disposed towards Christ, to offer one prayer or do one small deed for the love of God, it is an important step in the right direction. The least act on their part may open the way to the greater graces they need so much. . . .

"Monsignor Fearns," Keller went on, "replied in three words: 'Safe, sound and good.' And he underlined the word 'good.' " Keller's final words (quoted at the start of this chapter) were a challenge to the conscience of his correspondent.

Potentially most serious in its ramifications for the Christophers was an anonymous inquiry from the Vatican that was sent to Considine by the Apostolic Delegate, Archbishop Cicognani. Considine wrote (5/20/52):

Confidential memo *exclusively* to General and Vicar General: Archbishop Cicognani enlists me to serve as liaison in conveying to you this request for a report to be prepared personally by the General and Vicar General, to be typed by an individual of complete trust, and to be kept from the general files of the Society.

His Excellency . . . is keenly aware . . . that the mere fact of an inquiry from the Vatican implies to many people a criticism. Hence he asks that you permit him to insist that you in no way make reference to this inquiry in speaking to Father Keller until such time as His Excellency and you may feel it advisable.

His Excellency read to me a communication from the Secretariat of State. Father Keller, the letter said, is known at the Vatican as a priest of zeal and his work is looked upon favorably; however, a complaint has been received by the Holy Father that Father Keller issues an invitation to all to join him regardless of religious confession. The Secretariat of State asks the Delegate to send him a documentation on the work and, specifically, to determine if at the proper times and in proper fashion Father Keller makes a distinction between Catholic and non-Catholic.

In particular the Delegate asks for:

1. A statement prepared in duplicate on the origin, nature and development of the Christopher movement; in particular, explain its relations with Cardinal Spellman, the place of his office, the attitude of members of the Hierarchy, especially of Cardinal Mooney.

2. Two sets of Father Keller's books with date of the *imprimatur* of each; two sets of the principal literature of the Christopher movement.

All of this was prepared by T. S. Walsh and sent by Lane to Cicognani within three weeks. The letter mentioned that the Christophers had "been attacked by Father Leonard Feeney, the former Jesuit priest of Boston, who refused to obey his superiors in preaching on the question of no salvation outside the Church." Lane also noted a criticism from the *Christian Unitarian Register*, which referred to the Christophers as an "effective agency for spreading Roman Catholic propaganda." *The Nation* article was also referred to.

Lane assured Cicognani that Spellman had always been "fatherly and helpful," and that Keller frequently consulted with Mooney, who "has always shown a kindly interest in the idea." Lane summed up his assessment: "I am satisfied that Father Keller does make the necessary distinction between Catholic and non-Catholic, at the proper times and in the proper fashion."

Rome was not built in a day, nor does it respond in a week. About a year later on May 12, 1953, Spellman sent Maryknoll a copy of a letter he had written to Cicognani in response to the May 6 inquiry from the Delegate on the matter:

I wish to say that I can see no valid objection to the Christopher movement and I know personally that through the example, personality and preaching of Father Keller many indifferent Catholics have become good Catholics and many good Catholics have become truly apostolic. The Christopher movement has likewise attracted the attention of non-Catholics to the apostolicity of the Catholic Church and this has resulted both in conversions to Catholicism and a friendlier attitude and interest in matters relating to the Church.

Father Keller, the founder of the movement, is a Maryknoll priest and he serves under the supervision of the Vicar General of his own Order, Father Walsh, the Rector of our Seminary, who reviews the books and other literature published by the Christophers, and Monsignor Maguire, the Chancellor of the Archdiocese of New York, who supervises the financial aspects of the Christopher activities.

If there are any definite suggestions to be made, I shall be pleased to convey the expression of them to Father Keller who is, in my opinion, a zealous, humble and docile priest.

Naturally I do not know the purpose of this query but, to avoid the possibility of misunderstanding, I would say that, if there is any idea of the Holy See issuing any document concerning the Christophers, I would like to be heard before any action is taken to avoid the sensational and harmful repercussions to the Church which were occasioned by the general condemnation of membership in Rotary Clubs.

That was the end of it. The only concrete action that was taken by Keller's superiors was the formal setting up of the Cardinal's Committee for the Christophers, noted earlier.

An attack on Keller was made by David Gordon, a convert to Catholicism, who on September 23, 1954, wrote to Lane:

> Perhaps you will find the enclosed copy of letter [sic] interesting. I am contemplating getting together a petition to the Holy Office at Rome against Father Keller and his Christophers. I think I can prove from his own literature that this thing is accursed of God—a veritable conduit for the proliferation of the poison of Indifferentism and Secularism to Catholic souls.
>
> It seems to me too—and I propound this to Your Excellency in utmost respect and reverence—that a noble order like the Maryknoll Fathers which furnished martyrs for Christ would quickly scotch Keller whose central [sic] effect is to softpedal Jesus Christ for the sake of the primacy of politics.
>
> I know that you "need money," etc. But at this blasphemous expense?

David Gordon had written a letter to Monsignor Fearns four years earlier (5/1/49) which is worth quoting:

> There is being peddled to people all over America, a "Christopher prayer" composed by Rev. James Keller of the Maryknoll Fathers. This so-called "prayer" (like the Christopher organization) is deliberately composed to avoid any and all Catholic reference or connection. Father Keller, operating on a Confucian motto, openly believes in preaching "Americanism and Democracy without reference to Christ or Creed."
>
> Will you, reverend Monsignor, please advise me in the enclosed stamped self-addressed envelope, whether this "prayer" has the canonical approval of the Censor of the Archdiocese of New York?

It was the famous prayer for peace of St. Francis of Assisi.

* * *

Keller's critics held contradictory views about the purposes of his movement. Certain secularists believed he was seeking political domination by the Roman Catholic Church. Hard-line Catholics felt he was taking liberties with doctrine, or omitting unpalatable elements of Catholic teaching. (He did not emphasize those teachings that were hard for moderns to accept, but much of what he left out—such as the traditional teaching on Church and State—was soon to be jettisoned by the Second Vatican Council.) The inquiry from the Vatican's Secretariat of State, though it caused nervousness at Maryknoll, was probably no more than a desire to obtain information about a priest who had developed a popular following.

Keller knew that anyone who led a life out of the ordinary would be subject to criticism. There were times when he was hurt by it, especially when it came from those close to him, but he minimized its effects by heeding the words of his own motto: he kept lighting candles when it would have been easier to curse the darkness.

·*18*·

The Search for a Successor

"The time seems to have come to lay plans for its [the Christophers'] continuance and even greater development after I am out of picture." James Keller

Despite all his years without serious illness, Keller was always concerned about his health. As a youth, he had been put on a milk diet because he was thought to have tuberculosis. Later, his personal letters to superiors made occasional reference to his state of near physical exhaustion. One reason for Keller's weariness was his non-stop schedule; another was his chronic low blood pressure. To help overcome his fatigue, he would try to get a couple of hours of extra sleep each night or spend a long weekend swimming at the Murrays' in Southampton. Each day after lunch he tried to get a half-hour's rest, for such times of repose also helped him to clear his mind and formulate new plans for "changing the world."

Keller watched his diet carefully, avoiding harmful fried foods and subsisting at lunchtime on a menu of raw fruits and vegetables. He never drank coffee after breakfast. Keller's concern for his health was reinforced by a fear that he would die before his work was finished. In the early 1950s, he repeatedly told his associates that he would die young.

Keller realized he couldn't keep up his vigorous pace forever. In the early days of the Christophers, he had thought the work would last only a few years. But the success he met with soon convinced him that he could keep spreading the Christopher message, as he put it, "until the cows come home." Each generation of Catholics and others of good will, he reasoned, needed the simple reminder

168

that God had a mission for every person. Since the need for such reminders was not likely to diminish in his lifetime, Keller eventually recognized that he would have to start looking for an understudy and successor.

The arrival of Edward Flannery from Providence, Rhode Island, in 1950 gave Keller a reliable assistant director, but it is doubtful if Keller ever looked on him as someone who would carry on after him. By his own account,[1] Flannery was a man of introspective and meditative cast of mind, unlike the extroverted and sociable Keller. Flannery recalled that "I always believed that the [Christopher idea] was not as simple as Jim made it. He resisted all efforts to make it more than a repetition of the formula with an addition of a new story. His trump card, of course, was that it worked and paid off."

Flannery's duties at the Christopher office were limited to occasional talks, research on such books as *All God's Children*, and the "three minutes a day" series, as well as some News Notes.

"I was not allowed very much on the upper level of management of the Christophers," said Flannery. And indeed, that was a realm reserved for Keller himself. In this respect, Keller was not an effective manager. He could attract bright and willing people, but he was not always successful in keeping them. As "a man in a hurry," he didn't take the time or have the inclination to make sure they understood what he was driving at, or how he shaped his message to achieve his goals. The general office staff, which usually included thirty to forty workers, had a high turnover—though this was probably normal for a nonprofit organization which did not pay as well as private business.

Because of his prolonged absences on speaking tours or making TV programs in Hollywood, Keller became a distant father figure to most of his staff. He treated his employees about the same way he treated his own family—amiably, but at arm's length. "The work," as he referred to it, kept Keller visible to a great number of people but remote from those who might have had a greater claim on his time and attention. For years, those who knew him thought that nobody could work closely with Keller. Charles Oxton, who did so much work on *You Can Change the World*, disproved this axiom, however, and there would be others at a future date.

In Keller's absence, the office was run by a small cadre of assistants—Florence Okazaki, Mary Sullivan, Dolores Criqui, and a few others. Another was Fred Sauter who handled the bookkeeping, maintenance, and personnel duties. To these people fell the thankless task of making things work, mollifying disgruntled employees, and seeing to it that Keller's wishes were carried out, even if it meant long hours for them.

On rare occasions, Keller would take a personal hand in office procedures. One summer day, in 1960, he grew furious when he discovered that the mail from contributors was more than three weeks behind schedule. Keller fired the whole staff of letter-writers—mostly wealthy college girls who considered their job "volunteer work." At such times, Keller resembled his father, whose losses of temper were rare but terrifying.

As the year 1955 approached, Bishop McVinney of Providence came to the conclusion that Flannery wasn't going anywhere at the Christophers, and therefore offered him the editorship of the diocesan newspaper, *The Providence Visitor*. Flannery jumped at the chance. The bishop gave Keller several months to find a replacement, and so began a game of musical chairs, in which one priest after another held the post of assistant director.

Keller first looked crosstown in Manhattan to the headquarters of the Paulist Fathers. The Paulists, founded by Isaac Hecker in the nineteenth century, had the reputation of being a thoroughly Americanized order, and one dedicated—as was Keller, in a sense—to the conversion of the country to Catholicism. In January 1955, Keller wrote to Father William Michell, superior of the Paulists:

> Even at the outset, we realized it [the Christophers] was not directly in the province of a foreign mission society such as Maryknoll. But it was felt that if it was started and proved its worth, the Paulists, Jesuits or some other apostolic group in this country might be disposed to provide for its continuance and development.

Michell met with his Council and agreed to try to select a suitable priest by the fall. He inquired about the sort of work a Paulist would be expected to do, what sort of remuneration he would receive, and the attitude of the Archdiocese of New York to such a move. Keller responded that the priest would work with him "in every phase of the work . . . especially on the creative side." As for the Chancery, he said that he had already mentioned the possibility to the Cardinal's Committee and had received their unanimous approval. "They [the Committee] are most generous and keep repeating that the function of the Committee is merely advisory and protective while leaving the direction of administration in our hands." On May 4, 1955, Michell wrote: "Without any definite commitment as to our permanent relationship with the work . . . I have selected Father Joseph Flynn, who is at present Director of the Information Center here at 59th Street. He is a capable young priest with sufficient experience to make him an asset in your work."

Flynn entered the Christopher scene in September 1956 and picked up where Flannery left off. It was a short-lived assignment. Though he was not a writer by training, one of the first things he was asked to do was to write the daily Christopher newspaper column. Keller felt that the ability to write in the "Christopher style" was a prerequisite for any possible successor. For example, a news story about a child in a Catholic school who forgave someone who had planted a bomb in an airplane that crashed into the institution became simply "a child in a school." Where Keller would downplay any reference to Catholicism, however, Flynn wanted to mention it. Nevertheless, Flynn gave valuable assistance to the Christophers during the production of five dramatic programs for TV that were filmed in Hollywood in October of that year, an experience he found challenging and rewarding. Flynn also visited TV program directors in such cities as San Francisco, Denver, and Washington, D.C., in an effort to secure free air time for Christopher programs. The young Paulist took a lively interest in the lives of the Christopher staff, as had Flannery before him, thus contributing to an improvement in office morale.

Keller and Flynn got along well, despite Flynn's preference for a clearer identification of the Christophers with the Catholic Church. Keller favored the indirect approach, whereby people would find their own way to the Church because of the good works of its members. This was in contrast to the "convert-maker" approach so popular in the fifties, which placed heavy emphasis on logical proofs of the Church's divine origins.

Flynn had a high regard for Christopher activities, but he soon saw that it was not really a Paulist project. For one thing, he estimated that it would take three or four of the society's priests to replace Keller, something the small group was in no position to do. Furthermore, Keller gave no indication that he was about to turn over the reins to anybody. It was the Flannery experience all over again, only this time it took place within a shorter time. By the early months of 1956, Flynn was in the process of withdrawing from the Christophers. There were no hard feelings, simply a recognition that the future of the Christophers lay elsewhere than with the Paulists.

With the departure of Flynn, Keller turned to Bishop John Wright of Worcester, Massachusetts, for a priest, and in April 1957, Father Robert Howes became Keller's assistant. The relationship between the two men was uneasy from the start. Maryknoll required that a priest must be in the Christopher office during any long absences of Keller from New York, and with Howes in the office, Keller was able to travel to Rome in September to attend the International Congress of the Laity. Keller wrote to Howes from Rome (9/19/57):

> After I return from Rome in a few weeks, I hope to acquaint you with the different specific ingredients that make for whatever effectiveness our television programs have at present and how we hope to increase their audience appeal.

Keller recommended that his new assistant spend most of his time reading the special letters that came in and reading Christopher literature. Then he added:

> If any doubt arises about our policy at any time, it would be best to check. Make note of any suggestions you may have for the improvement of the work. We can discuss them on my return. Please postpone everything which might involve the slightest deviation from our present policy.

Howes' tenure at the Christophers was brief. Wright confirmed the fact that the experiment had not succeeded in this letter (2/20/58) to Keller:

> I have your letter of February 17 and I am grateful for it. In the light of it, I am writing to Father Howes to say that I have

learned that his arrangements with the Christophers will ter-
minate on or before March 3 and that I am expecting word
from him. I deeply appreciate the spirit of your letter and, as
always, I wish you every blessing in the apostolate.

Keller next turned to the Jesuits. He wrote to Father Thomas
Henneberry, the provincial, in January 1958, who replied that
Keller's request would have to be reviewed by all nine of the other
American provincials and approved by the Jesuit Father General.
"Since I do not wish to raise false hopes," he wrote, "I must say
that I believe Father General would reply that we already have
more than we can do in promoting the Apostleship of Prayer and
the Sodalities."

Father Robert Gannon, former president of Fordham University
and a friend of Keller's, wrote to the latter with the half-serious
comment that a takeover by the Jesuits would probably snuff out
any spark of spontaneity and originality that the movement possessed.

Undaunted, Keller turned to the Oblates of St. Francis de Sales.
In April 1958, he met for two hours with Father William Buckley,
the provincial. But on May 5 Buckley wrote a kind but negative
reply, telling Keller that "we have decided that it would be impossible for us to assign a priest to you at this time. Frankly, one
of the reasons for this decision is that we cannot find the right man
to send you!"

The only recourse for the future of the Christophers was Maryknoll. As early as October 1956, Keller wrote Bishop Lane's successor as superior general, Father John Comber, asking him to "be
on the lookout for a Maryknoll priest, not vitally needed, who might
work with me."

A few weeks later, he renewed his reminder:

> An examination by the doctor not long ago gave me the good
> news that my health is tip-top, thank God. But in case I should
> get run over, dropped in the East River or deported, I feel I
> should make at least a suggestion regarding the continuity of
> Christopher work. After trying several padres, I would say that
> Father Joe Grassi stands out as the most interested and best
> equipped to carry on perchance I did shuffle off into eternity
> unexpectedly. He is, I realize, essential for the job he is doing

now at the Seminary [teaching Sacred Scripture]. But during the Summer and in the last couple of months he has had enough of a hand in the work to know the ropes and proved quite capable at it.

Comber did not think Grassi was the man for the job, so discussions continued between Keller and the Maryknoll Council, especially with Father John F. Donovan, the new Vicar General, who proved to be most sympathetic and influential. On May 24, 1958, Donovan sent a memo to the Council. After repeating the usual objections that would be involved in a closer relationship between the two organizations, he pointed out:

1. We have 32 priests of the Society in parish work; four in the Armed Services; we have "mission" parishes in New York City, Chicago and Los Angeles; we have other Maryknollers engaged in work only indirectly connected with foreign missions.

2. The Constitutions #26 and #27 provide for members doing work outside their mission region and "work outside the Society."

3. Would there be danger to our reputation if, without providing for its continuance, we let the successful movement drop? Would there be danger that it might be considered a Maryknoll "trick," to push in and arbitrarily withdraw?

4. Father Keller has succeeded pretty well in keeping Maryknoll out of the business up to now, although most people realize that he is a Maryknoll priest.

5. We should make sure that the Christopher movement remains an independent organization, formed with the approval of the Cardinal and under the direction of a Board of Directors named by the Cardinal of New York. Maryknoll might for the time being continue to supply the Director of the Christophers and we might add one assistant to assure the continuity of the movement.

6. In other words, Maryknoll would take the responsibility to supply limited personnel to do the work, and nothing more. This seems to have been Cardinal Spellman's idea of what he thought the relationship of Maryknoll should be to the Christophers.

This memo marked a turning point in Keller's relationship with Maryknoll. For the first time, serious consideration was being given to Keller's search for a successor—and the society's responsibility in the event of his demise. Maryknoll was also under pressure from the Cardinal's Committee to provide an understudy and even successor for Keller. Meanwhile, Keller had already found his man— Graham McDonnell, a newly ordained priest who was living at the 39th Street house while attending the Graduate School of Journalism at Columbia University. On January 22, 1959, Keller wrote to his Maryknoll superior asking for McDonnell.

Then, possibly at Keller's prompting, Spellman stepped into the picture (1/23/59) with a letter to Comber:

> Monsignor Maguire has given me the report of the recent meeting of the priests designated to assist Father Keller in his apostolate. Father Keller's work is so very important and the results so consoling that I really believe provision should be made for the work to be carried on.
>
> I have been told that Father Graham McDonnell of Maryknoll is familiar with the Christopher idea and sympathetic to it, and I would appreciate it if you and your Council would give consideration to the proposal that Father McDonnell be appointed assistant to Father Keller, with the same provision for leave of absence which Father Keller has at the present time.
>
> While it is not strictly speaking a Maryknoll work, nevertheless the Christopher movement falls within the wide scope of Maryknoll's objectives and will continue to add to Maryknoll's prestige and, therefore, Maryknoll's influence.

The Cardinal's word had its effect. On April 24, 1959, an ecstatic Keller wrote to Comber:

> The morning mail brought great news from you and the Council! Will keep it confidential till tomorrow. I am at a loss to express my deep appreciation for this wonderful evidence of confidence in the missionary potential of the Christopher idea and your generosity in sparing such a good man as Father Gra-

ham—I'll try to make up by prayers for you and the Council in the never-ending problems that confront you.

The search for a successor had ended, at least for the moment. More important, Maryknoll had recognized its responsibility to see that it would not let the Christopher movement "go down the drain."

·19·

Fresh Winds from Europe

"The priest must have had a seminary training that adequately equips him to proclaim the Gospel message in such a dynamic way that the follower of Christ will catch its apostolic implications and apply them by prayer, word and deed."
                                                            James Keller

The arrival of Graham McDonnell at the Christopher headquarters strengthened Keller's ties to Maryknoll. Those in the society who resented Keller's leaving promotion work fifteen years before were now outnumbered by dozens of younger men to whom this meant little or nothing. They saw Keller as part of the American church scene, a priest whose ideas were practical guides to stirring up the lay apostolate on the missions. John F. Donovan, the architect of this rapprochement, invited Keller to participate once again in the Development (promotion) Department's monthly meetings, which Keller was only too happy to do.

The son of a Detroit journalist, McDonnell brought a more contemporary style to Christopher writings. News Notes such as "How to Be a Leader," "How Parliamentary Law Protects You," and "Good Government Begins With You" showed the effect of McDonnell's writing skill, and they were extremely popular. Even the graphics were improved. Beginning about this time (1960), the News Notes became an entity unto themselves, whereas previously they had served more as a public relations newsletter for other Christopher activities. Keller himself began to put in more time on the research and composition of the Notes, the result being a more tightly written publication that had an overall unity and punch it did not always possess in the past.

McDonnell also took on the task of revising the book, *Government Is Your Business*, which was reissued in time for the 1960 presidential campaign. It sold briskly.

In the field of promotion, McDonnell was not an unqualified success. Having grown up in a staunchly pro-union family, he was distressed by Keller's familiarity with the wealthy, especially those who represented the ruling oligarchy of Detroit industrial society. His class-consciousness—in addition to the almost universal desire of Maryknollers to go to the foreign missions—led Keller to decide that this was not the replacement he had hoped for. Keller already had his eye on someone else. That person was myself.

I had followed McDonnell at the Columbia Graduate School of Journalism, living at the Maryknoll residence during my year of study. There I encountered Keller regularly at morning prayers, breakfast, and sometimes at supper. McDonnell and I had become good friends, and in the course of many conversations, he painted an enthusiastic picture of the possibilities of the Christopher idea. McDonnell predicted that I would take his place—and he was right. When the mission assignments were published in May, McDonnell was sent to Japan, where he works today as a missioner with the Good Shepherd movement, an organization with similarities to the Christophers. I was assigned to the Christophers. With my own sights set on a mission assignment overseas, I took the news with mixed feelings. My confreres at Maryknoll wished me good luck, but with little expectation that I would last any longer than my predecessors. The Cultivation (public relations) Department, under the direction of John Considine and Albert Nevins, was willing to have me collaborate with Keller "to pick his brains" and learn whatever I could for the benefit of Maryknoll in the United States and overseas.

To everyone's surprise, Keller and I got along extremely well. Instead of putting me off in a corner—his usual practice with new-comers—he soon moved my desk into his office, right next to his. I was able to pick up the "Christopher style" in a matter of days and was soon writing newspaper columns to Keller's satisfaction. He and I collaborated on News Notes in painstaking line-by-line sessions. The result was that their upward swing in popularity continued. My grasp of Keller's objective—"to make everyone a missioner"—grew as I struggled with the writing process during the hot summer of 1960. I helped him put into final form a book he had been laboring over for several years. Titled *Change the World from Your Parish*, it was the first explicitly "Catholic" book Keller had written since *The Priest and a World Vision* (1946).

Now that the burden of writing was more evenly distributed, we turned to writing special Christopher Notes "for priests and religious." Among these were "Love—or Be Destroyed" and "Christopher Tips for Lay Apostles," which were distributed through parishes to the Catholic laity. In them, we urged our coreligionists to get out of their "spiritual ghetto" and become involved in the fast-changing, technological world symbolized by the Kennedy era. It was a heady and happy time. Keller had found a disciple who could write and who could keep up with him during his twelve-hour days. We shared the same dreams, hopes, and laughter.

I knew I had reached the "upper level of management" in September 1961 when Keller invited me to join him for a few days at the home of John and Barbara Newington,[1] at whose Greenwich, Connecticut, home he stayed on weekends. Between work sessions on News Notes, one called "Gear Yourself for a Fast-Changing World," we swam in the Newingtons' pool and set aside time for prayers. For the first time, I saw Keller out of his clerical dress, wearing a comfortable blue sport shirt. Here, I began to see, was his real family. From then on, Keller involved me wholeheartedly in the writing of News Notes, and listened to my judgment on this and other matters. By the following spring, I had written Number 120 myself, "If You Won't—Who Will?" It was the first of the News Notes not written by Keller himself.

Over Keller's strong objections, I was reassigned, in June 1962, to do editorial work with Maryknoll's Cultivation Department, and during my absence Maryknoll honored its commitment to provide a priest-assistant by sending Father Walter Kelleher, just back from Japan, to work with Keller. This interruption of my Christopher work lasted but one year. In May 1963, Keller welcomed me back, and began to make sure I received a thorough apprenticeship. In 1964, he shared the spotlight with me by making me cohost of the Christopher TV Program. He had me alternate with him in the writing and recording of one-minute radio spots, which were broadcast daily on more than 2,000 stations. Keller shared equal billing with me as coauthor of the "three-minute-a-day" books, starting in 1964. And he took me with him to Hollywood to make Christopher TV films and to visit benefactors across the country, where he introduced me as his future successor.

* * *

Another person who played a key role in Keller's life during the late fifties to the late sixties was Father Prudencio Damboriena, a Spanish Jesuit whom Keller met during the World Congress of the Lay Apostolate, held in Rome in 1957. Keller found the congress long on rhetoric and short on practical applications, but meeting Damboriena, dean of the Pontifical Gregorian University's department of Missiology, made the trip worthwhile. This short, stocky Basque, who had served briefly in China and then was transferred to Latin America, knew many international theologians, especially among the Jesuits. When he met Keller, he was compiling a massive study of the inroads being made in the traditionally Catholic continent of South America by fundamentalist Protestant sects from the North. Damboriena tried to alert the authorities in Rome that only a vigorous lay apostolate, along the lines of the Christophers, could bring about the resurgence of a Catholic faith in tune with the times. Always sensitive to the charge that the Christopher movement was sketchy in its theology, Keller employed the erudition and missionary experience of Damboriena to bring out the missionary principles he felt were at the heart of the work. Beginning with the summer of 1958, Damboriena came to New York each year and helped establish the theological structure for the book, *Change the World from Your Parish*. It was through the Jesuit that Keller secured an *imprimatur* for the book from Aloysius Cardinal Traglia, provicar of Rome. It was a rare distinction for a book by an American, adding to its prestige.

Damboriena's concern for the future of the Catholic Church in Latin America was a stimulus to Keller to begin a series of Christopher News Notes, called *Ecos Cristóforos*, in Spanish. *Ecos*, which consisted mainly of translations and adaptations of the English versions, was sent without charge six times a year to individuals and church groups, many of whom had been requesting such a service. It filled a gap made by the lack of contemporary literature from a Catholic source. Keller turned to Peter Grace for financial help in the mailing and printing of *Ecos Cristóforos*, and the Grace Foundation gave substantial help to the project in the years to come.

Change the World from Your Parish was translated by Damboriena and published in Mexico City in 1967. It went into three printings of 10,000 each, a good sale for this kind of book.

The purpose of *Change the World from Your Parish*, a 468-page paperback, was stated at the outset:

> The aim of this Christopher handbook is to encourage every member of every parish to be an apostle in applying the love and truth of Christ to a world that "was made through Him," but that always falters and founders when it "knows Him not." (John 1:10)

The volume contained thirty-three chapters, from "Forty Challenging Years Ahead" to "This Way to Heaven." It discussed the Incarnation, the Mass, the natural law—its theological underpinnings—but also dealt with specific practical matters, such as working within organizations, using parliamentary law, good government, better schools, the importance of writing, the sanctity of marriage, and pointers for parents and teenagers. It was Keller's answer to the vagueness he had found at the World Congress of the Laity. And it was based explicitly on principles of Catholic teaching, authenticated by theological experts, which had received little emphasis in most parishes, not to say seminaries. The first printing was 100,000, and the book was eventually translated into Spanish. Damboriena's enthusiasm for the concept "every Catholic a missioner" could not fail to impress those who had considered Keller something of a lightweight.

* * *

Through Peter and Margie Grace, Keller became acquainted in 1960 with one of the foremost theologians of the lay apostolate—Leo Cardinal Suenens of Malines, Belgium. Suenens read the manuscript of *Change the World from Your Parish* and wrote back:

> It was a joy to read the manuscript . . . . My impression is excellent and I have no corrections to suggest. I see that you stress strongly the importance of the parish and I think you are right. . . . I am sure the handbook will be very helpful. People

need to be convinced that he [sic] can do something practical. It is so important to answer the question: *"quomodo fiet istud?"* ["how can this be done?"] but you did it.

When the Second Vatican Council began in 1962, Cardinal Suenens, a leader of the "progressive" wing of the bishops, invited Keller to join him in Rome to speak to bishops, theologians, and seminarians. The invitation was regretfully declined. News Notes, television, and daily Christopher columns were taking too much of Keller's time.

Around the same time Damboriena wrote to the now-Bishop Comber who was in Rome for the first session of the Second Vatican Council:

> As you know, it has been my privilege, all along these years, to watch closely (and, I must say, at times critically) the way the movement carries on its work. I believe, honestly, that Father Keller's achievement is, in general, excellent. . . . But the fact that has impressed me most has been the reaction of the common people . . . as seen in the mail coming to him from all over the world. These spontaneous and sincere letters from Bishops, priests, seminarians, religious, Protestant pastors and common folks are the best tribute to the Christophers. . . . The long letters sent from far-off mission countries or the short postcards scrapped [sic] by a good housekeeper in a Middle West city, show the possibilities of missionary work hidden in so many people who would like to do something for the Lord, but earnestly ask to be told how to do it.

Damboriena continued:

> It is my conviction that the Christopher spirit can become a powerful instrument of modern missionary apostolate. It gives to our whole mission work a new dimension and a universal outlook so much needed in our times. The movement is proving its worth as a service to the universal Church in missionary lands as well as in the homeland. And I am sure its effectiveness will increase as the institution gets the personnel required for its needs. In this I am thinking specially of Latin America, where we need badly the spirit of the movement in order to keep those countries within the fold of the Church.

Damboriena urged the Maryknoll superior to assure that the Christophers would not die in the event of the retirement of its founder but that Maryknoll would "protect the continuity of the endeavor by supplying needed personnel."

At the time of Damboriena's correspondence with Comber, Walter Kelleher was Keller's assistant. He gave this account of his year at the Christophers:

> I had just come back from six years working as a young Maryknoll missionary priest in Japan, but Jim expected me to buckle right down and work with him. He set a fast pace, every day, all day. I learned a lot from him. But not neatness. His desk was a foot deep in old newspapers, etc., but he knew where everything was at all times. He was also generous to a fault, always giving everyone the benefit of the doubt. . . . We wrote his autobiography, *To Light a Candle*, the year I worked with Jim, and I repeat the comment I made at that time: the best book would have been the one that wasn't printed. To explain, I was in great admiration of the way Jim had overcome so many obstacles, but in charity, he omitted all that. Building up the Christophers was not an easy task, and he and it were not always appreciated by some people.[2]

Appreciated or not, Keller never looked back. With encouragement from Cardinal Suenens and practical help from Damboriena, Keller convened a conference to put the Second Vatican Council's principles to work where he felt they would do the most good—in the world's seminaries. Keller was convinced that an active laity could not emerge unless it was guided by priests who knew how to stimulate the "apostolic potential" of their people.

The Christopher office was no longer housed in rented quarters. In 1961, Keller had acquired a building at 16th East 48th Street, the very building in which Julia Ward had allowed him to set up his first Maryknoll office back in 1933. By this time, I was back at my Christopher desk, eager to play a role that would give the movement some theological weight.

The first Christopher Study Week took place in July 1963. About a dozen priests attended, among them, Father Edward Malone, dean of Maryknoll Seminary, and two Spanish Jesuits, friends of Father Damboriena. They were Alfonso Nebreda of Japan and José

Calle from the Philippines. Keller proved a superior organizer. He insisted that all papers be sent to him in advance and distributed to all participants before the meeting. The conference time was spent in discussing each paper in turn and, on the final day, formulating conclusions.

In his opening statement, Keller told the theologians:

> Our purpose in these conferences is to rediscover the apostolic (missionary) elements already contained in the deposit of faith, in Holy Scripture, in the writings of the Fathers and in every tract of sacred theology. Inasmuch as all our theology revolves around the mystery of the Incarnation, which is the love of God coming to men and extending to the uttermost parts of the earth, we can be sure that these divine truths contain all the power needed to generate this dynamism in candidates for the priesthood. Only when there are zealous priests in every parish endowed with these ideals, can we hope to train new generations of laymen to fulfill their missionary tasks in every field. May the Holy Spirit find in us ready instruments to make a contribution, however limited, during this new era of increased pastoral concern inaugurated by the Ecumenical Council.

The group worked hard and long in a crowded conference room barely made tolerable in the summer heat by a window air conditioner. But no one complained, to Keller at least. One participant, excited by the breaking of new ground, called this meeting "an act of collective courage." Another pointed out that Christianity was a message, not a "system," and that the message was summed up in the person of Christ. A third pointed out that Protestants should not be seen as "adversaries," but should be welcomed for the insights their theologians had brought to truths insufficiently proclaimed in Catholic teaching.

The conclusions that came out of the conference called for practical training for seminarians to give them "an organized and guided experience in pastoral action." They stressed the apostolic dimension in all theology and the integration of biblical studies with liturgy. These conclusions, running no more than 2,000 words, were published and sent to every bishop, priest, and seminary in the United States and to many in other countries. Reactions to this first attempt to make practical application of some of the teachings of the Vatican Council were swift and positive.

Archbishop Denis Hurley of Durban, South Africa, a progressive bishop at the Council, wrote (8/23/63):

> The ideas expressed in these findings are magnificent and I sincerely hope that you have kindled the spark in the United States that is going to spread into every Seminary and Catholic faculty and that will have repercussions, in fact, all over the world. When an idea begins to take practical shape in the United States, we can usually expect results.

No less enthusiastic was Bishop John Mark Gannon of Erie, Pennsylvania:

> I am very impressed with your meeting. . . . I believe the whole seminary course and practice should be recast to meet the zeal and goodness of the modern priest, who is willing to do apostolic work but is frozen by so much abstraction and theological disputes of past centuries. . . . Theology is not an abstraction— but dynamic and practical. Young American priests love Christian apostolic work. They quiet down when it comes to abstract theses. I am unhappy with the young *ordinandi* in our seminaries who lack the practical tools for spreading our Lord's mission on earth. The sad record of American converts is evidence of this statement.

Archbishop MacDonald of Edmonton, Alberta, said:

> You and your associates will be rewarded . . . for directing attention to the part which seminary training should play in making priests and people fully aware that God demands more than to merely hold what we have. The Church is a living organism and must grow. This can be done only in its members, the men and women who comprise it, going out themselves into those parts of the world that know not Christ, and making Him known by their charity and efficiency.

The second Christopher Study Week, held in July 1964, played host to an impressive galaxy of the world's leading theologians, from both religious orders and diocesan seminaries.[3] The group issued a much longer (5,500-word) summary of conclusions, and published the papers delivered at the conference in a fifty-cent paperback, "Apostolic Renewal in the Seminary." This became a basic text for the renewal of seminary training throughout the world, with editions appearing in several languages.

The Jesuit quarterly, *Theological Studies*, devoted three pages to its review of the book.[4] Considered with two other works on seminary training, the Christopher book was introduced with this comment: "The major shortcoming of the two books reviewed so far is that, although both stress the need of a revision of the seminary curriculum, neither shows concretely how this goal might be achieved. For suggestions along this line, the Keller-Armstrong paperback . . . may profitably be consulted." The review concluded by commending the various authors for "helpful suggestions for seminary professors anxious to intensify the pastoral thrust of their courses."

An Australian priest[5] said that the book landed in the regional seminary of Waaga Waaga "like a bombshell." Copies were eagerly passed around by seminary students longing for release from the confining seminary curriculum. The seminary authorities, firmly rooted in another century, were disturbed by the fresh winds of change, even if they came from Rome. The students' revolt was put down, but not before many of them were infected by the thought that the Church could indeed change with the times. ·

Avery Dulles of Woodstock referred to the 1964 meeting as "almost a conversion experience. I was much more hesitant about the thing before we met. It just seemed that the Holy Spirit was there, a real consensus was reached and we all resonated with one another in a really remarkable way." About Keller's role, he said:

> Keller was the catalyst. He didn't really push any ideas of his own that I can remember. Although obviously his concerns about the dimension of lay involvement and the distance between the seminary and the laity did become known. It seemed to me he was a very objective chairman. He simply recognized people in order and allowed the process to unfold. And it did. It was one of the best meetings of that kind I've ever attended. . . . The combination of the two [study weeks] cer-

tainly started a lot of people thinking about revisions of seminary life, the seminary curriculum, liturgy, spiritual direction, and so forth. Tremendous changes were soon to take place in practically all seminaries in the country.

The third and last study week began on July 3, 1965. The Christophers issued a thirty-page booklet (first printing: 120,000 copies) on the conclusions, based on the Vatican Council's first three documents: on the Church, the Sacred Liturgy, and Ecumenism. Father Frederick McManus, one of the participants and a member of the Bishops' Commission on the Liturgical Apostolate, wrote to Keller on August 9 that "I have nothing but admiration for your efforts in sponsoring such an important gathering. Besides which, as I mentioned before, it was an extremely enjoyable experience."

Not all the reactions were positive. In Los Angeles in November 1965, Keller paid a courtesy call on Cardinal McIntyre and received "the most thorough tongue-lashing of my life." The cardinal thought that Keller had no business sticking his nose into seminary training and forbade him to send copies of the study week conclusions to any of the priests in his archdiocese. Keller emerged from the meeting a shaken man, but quickly recovered. The cardinal's instructions were followed.

On the other hand, Keller received a letter on the third study week from Archbishop John J. Maguire, Coadjutor of New York (11/4/65):

> Monsignor O'Brien, before leaving for a short visit to Rome, returned the galley sheets of your report on the Third Christopher Study Week with this note: "I consider the pamphlet not only without objections but very good!"

A fourth study week to be based on the Council's Constitution on the Church in the Modern World, a natural for the Christophers, was planned for the summer of 1966. But Keller had been disappointed by the mediocre quality of the papers in the 1965 study week and decided not to publish them, or to go ahead with another meeting. In the wake of the Council, unrest and division were beginning to cause turmoil in Church life, and it may be that Keller harbored secret doubts about the advisability of continuing these avant garde meetings. His shattering experience with McIntyre may have been a factor. So too was the reason he actually gave: the launching of Christopher half-hour programs, to replace the easier quarter-hour shows he had been doing of late, was going to take too much of his time. Planning and carrying out another international theological conference was not something he could delegate. And he was beginning to feel the burdens of age. Keller was soon to be sixty-six.

The head of the Maryknoll Sisters, Mother Mary Coleman, asked the Christophers to sponsor a conference on the renewal of convent life, along the lines of Cardinal Suenens' provocative book, *The Nun in the World*. Religious sisters were leaving the classrooms in search of close involvement with the poor, often living in small rented apartments instead of convents. The project was full of possibilities, given Keller's skill at making fresh ideas palatable to church authorities, but it contained hidden dangers as well. Feeling he would be over his head in this unfamiliar territory, Keller politely declined.

Keller was basically a conservative man, a reformer perhaps, but a gradualistic one. He believed that people and institutions do not change through confrontation. The turmoil in the Church and the antiwar protests of the late sixties left him stunned. It was a difficult period for Keller, who found it hard, for example, to accept the new liturgical practices. After more than forty years of celebrating Mass in Latin, usually in private, he could not be expected to take to the vernacular and other sweeping changes. But he made himself accept the Church's decrees and eventually grew to like both the "new Mass" and the English breviary. Nevertheless, at times, he wondered where it would all lead. To one non-Catholic friend[6] he confessed that he hoped he would die while he could still die a Catholic! He welcomed change but not, in his phrase, "too much, too soon."

The picture of Keller in the mid-sixties was that of a rapidly aging man, gamely trying to keep abreast. He worked with José Calle, an acknowledged catechetical expert, and Maryknoll Sister Julia Bertrand, who had studied at the *Lumen Vitae* Institute in Brussels, to produce a "Christopher Catechism." It was to be a scriptural handbook, showing from the Bible how God called people individually to fulfill their mission in the world. The most successful chapter concerned the call of Moses, a reluctant prophet if there ever was one. Keller and I worked on this chapter for weeks, hoping it would be a model for Calle and Bertrand to follow. It had humor, pathos, and a contemporary style. The trouble was, we couldn't sustain that high level, and neither could they. Keller and I had neither the academic background nor the time to write a ground-breaking "apostolic" catechism and our two experts started going off in another direction. Keller suggested to Calle that he take what he had written and use it in the Philippines, where Calle headed the East Asian Pastoral Institute [EAPI] in Manila. It never became a book, although some of the chapters appeared in the EAPI's magazine, *Teaching All Nations*. Calle felt that the effort was not lost: "A number of the insights acquired during those laborious sessions at the Christopher's office were incorporated in the Christian Communities Program, launched in 1968 and implemented in many dioceses of East Asia."[7]

Keller never got the catechism he wanted, but his ideas on the lay apostolate, through Calle's efforts, had an influence on perhaps 1,500 priests, sisters, and lay leaders who have taken the courses sponsored by the East Asian Pastoral Institute. Many of those who took the course were Maryknollers.

Tired though he was, Keller never stopped trying to change the world. He corresponded with Father Pedro Arrupe, newly elected superior of the 30,000-member Society of Jesus. At Arrupe's invitation, Keller flew to Rome in February 1966 to offer the Jesuit, who had been a missionary in Japan, some suggestions on how the Order could revitalize both Church and world. In a letter he gave to Arrupe, Keller said:

> The Society of Jesus could make an outstanding contribution in implementing the directives of the Second Vatican Council if it would lay greater emphasis on the need for personal involvement on the part of our laity. Your Society might do more than any other group in the Church to prevent the Council accomplishments from suffering the same fate that often befalls papal encyclicals—admired by many, read by some and acted on only by a few.

It was all true, but probably not of much help to Arrupe, except in an inspirational sense. The Jesuit leader did much to change the direction of the Order from the education of the rich to identification with the poor in their struggle for liberation. But Keller's influence on the Jesuits was probably through Christopher books and News Notes in Spanish and English, which were sent regularly to hundreds of them throughout the world, rather than by his exhortations to Arrupe.

During Maryknoll's General Chapter meeting of 1966, Keller made the same basic plea to the assembled delegates that he had made to Arrupe. He won a respectful hearing for his past accomplishments, but little more. In fact this meeting simply set the scene for one final effort to resolve the ambiguities of Maryknoll's relationship with the Christophers.

·20·

Tapering Off

"The years are ticking off one by one."   James Keller

The year 1966 was decisive for the Christophers on several fronts. The delegates who met for the Maryknoll Chapter that year showed the reformist urge to solve all the problems of the society—including the clarification of the murky relationship of Maryknoll to the Christophers. Not everyone was friendly to Keller. Father Raymond Hill, an admirer of Keller, recalled his own efforts to keep the Christophers independent:

> It was during the '66 Chapter that I became aware of the strong anti-Jim attitudes of some members of the Society. An unofficial committee was set up to make a recommendation to the Chapter. As I recall it, it was loaded against him, or so it seemed to me. Somehow I got on it and joined with those who appreciated Jim's work. We were able to halt the thrust that seemed to want to read him out of the Society and ended up with a compromise, leaving it up to Jim and the future Council to decide whether it would become part of Maryknoll's Social Communications Department or go independent and work directly under the New York Archdiocese.

The delegates, in their desire for ecclesiastical neatness, seemed to be unaware that these options had been explored—and rejected—years before.

Keller, knowing that the delegates would soon be back on the missions and recognizing that his substantive dealings would be with the newly elected superior general, Father John McCormack, and his Council, played for time. He did not want to upset what he called the "delicate balance" that had served Maryknoll and left him free to pursue his goals. He reacted with surprise when he read McCormack's letter of November 1966:

> The place of the Christopher movement within Maryknoll has been a hotly discussed issue within the Society for the past decade. In a matter of such complexity, I have no wish to be precipitate. . . . I will welcome any thoughts which this letter may stimulate.

My own feelings were of dismay. I felt the delegates were trying to smother a lively and productive organization under a layer of controls that could snuff it out. Keller was simpler and wiser. He didn't know, or didn't choose to remember, that his movement had been a "hotly discussed issue." He just wanted to be left alone. Together we drafted a cautious reply that opted vaguely for some kind of further Maryknoll connection.

The Social Communications Department, now headed by Father Albert Nevins,[1] was no more eager to get entangled with the Christophers than Keller himself, though for different reasons. Nevins thought it had been a mistake to let Keller start the movement in the first place, and that for Maryknoll to take further responsibility for the Christophers would be to perpetuate that original mistake. The delegates had proposed a wedding for which neither partner was anxious.

Over the next two years, a few meetings were held in which Keller and I plied Maryknoll's representatives with good food and drink—and which led to nothing. It was, in a way, Keller's final triumph.

As Keller aged, he asked himself whether he was jeopardizing the movement by not providing more effectively for its future. He saw men of his generation holding onto their positions for dear life, and he did not want to make the same mistake. He often wondered out loud whether he was holding the Christopher idea back by his own "limited vision."

If Keller's vision was limited, it was seldom apparent to those who worked with him. He continued to dream dreams into his sixties, even as his energy reached a plateau and later went into rapid decline.

One dream Keller realized in the early 1960s was the launching of Christopher Leadership Courses. Ever since the Career Guidance School plan was nipped in the bud in 1949, he had nourished the hope that someday he would revive this plan in some form. His friend, Father Thomas Bresnahan, was enjoying much success in Detroit with the Gabriel Richard courses, which had a Christopher genesis and used many Christopher materials. Several of Bresnahan's former instructors, who now resided in the New York area, offered to help the courses get started. But it was June Guncheon, a communication specialist and consultant to many large corporations, who gave wings to the Christopher course. She laid out the seven-session course and provided a teacher's guide that would enable a relatively inexperienced volunteer teacher to get surprising results out of tongue-tied participants. Talks were kept short— thirty seconds to two minutes—and comments were kept positive and short. It was a case of "learn by doing." Through advertisements in the *New York Times* and diocesan newspapers, the course drew classes of between twenty and twenty-five, often running three nights a week. When it became difficult to find volunteer instructors, Keller hired Robert L. Montgomery, a communication consultant from Minneapolis, to run the course.

Not satisfied with starting a course for Christophers in the heart of the world's communication capital, Keller wanted to package it for global distribution. Using June Guncheon's materials, he produced a handbook called *How to Be a Leader*, which could be used anywhere—in the home, church, social organization, or office. Published in 1963, the book—which was unique in that it did not need a trained instructor to present its ideas—reached the public at the right time. More than 300,000 copies were sold and distributed over the next few years. The book was translated into Spanish, Portuguese, and Japanese, as well as published in English in India and the Philippines. Since fear of public speaking is an obstacle to involvement in the spheres of Christopher influence, Keller saw his communication course as the first step in leadership. He once expressed his regret that "in all those television programs, all those films, I never had anyone to help me. I wish I'd had some professional coaching." What he never got for himself, he was offering (in the best way he knew) to people all over the United States, as well as in Africa, Asia, and Latin America, where the book was widely used by missionaries and lay leaders. To a degree, at least, it made up for the canceling of his career guidance program years before.

The year 1963 was also the one in which Keller published his autobiography, *To Light a Candle*. Because of Keller's self-effacement and charity, the book told little about the man and even less about the people who had made his road to achievement so difficult. Lacking any real conflict, the volume sold only modestly by comparison with other Christopher books.

Keller was no longer traveling the way he once did. He needed his weekends with John and Barbara Newington in Greenwich to rest and relax. Still, he spared no effort to perfect the News Notes. How I remember those hours spent struggling for the right phrase or the best way to organize a particular issue. One after another they rolled off the presses: "It's Your Government," "16 Tips for Potential Writers," "Change the World from Your Home," "How to Become an Effective Speaker," "The Hope of the Natural Law," "Work at Your Work," "Take a Stand for Decency," "World Hunger Can Be Overcome," "How to Strengthen Any Organization," "Apply the Bible to Modern Life." Each one represented dozens of hours of labor—followed by exhilaration when letters poured in by the thousands from people who found in these leaflets the spiritual nourishment they were not getting from their churches or anywhere else. The return of Jeanne Glynn, who rejoined the Christophers in 1964 after a four-year hiatus, added a third member to our creative writing team. Keller gradually relinquished more of the research and writing to Jeanne Glynn and me. She remembered Keller in these words:

> He was an old-fashioned man ahead of his time. He was a traditionalist who sought the new. He was a man of the world uncomfortable in it. Never devious, always discreet. He was a man of change who feared it. He was a man of conviction and indecision. He was a public figure and a personal enigma, an outspoken man, a shy man.[2]

Keller showed a shrewd sense of timing in 1965, when he first began to make Christopher television programs in color. He expanded the program to thirty minutes and, in concert with Jack Denove, devised a new format. Keller and I were the cohosts while Jeanne Glynn and I did most of the writing. June Guncheon's short segments on Christopher leadership were a popular feature of the program. The shows began to take on a more contemporary note, echoing the hopes and concerns of the sixties. Other religious organizations were buying time on TV. The Christophers held their own in major markets because of the regard that station directors had for Keller, because of the stars and personalities he persuaded to appear with him, and because the Christopher program was one of the first to use color.

Jack Denove died in April 1968. Despite the personal loss and what it could mean to Keller's work, the Christopher program had been solidly established and its popularity continued. Another innovation in television during the sixties was the development of videotape, and after Denove's death, the switch to tape was made. Unlike film, it could be reused, and thus the move represented a long-term saving of money. Tape was also easier to use and meant that the program could be made by directors who did not necessarily have a genius for film, but belonged to the new breed who worked well with videotape. Again, Keller's timing was right.

Keller was not a brick-and-mortar man, but he knew that his organization needed a modern building. The small structure at 16 East 48th Street was barely adequate. It was old and needed many repairs. In reality, it was only a stepping stone to the one he had had his eyes on all along—a solid, modern seven-story building at 12 East 48th Street. There were a few problems: the owner didn't want to sell; the Archdiocese wouldn't let him buy; and he didn't have the money.

The owner, Alfred Kaskel, eventually changed his mind. Keller secured from the Archdiocese permission to be given a building. And he called upon Newington to be the lucky doner. Newington bought Kaskel's building in September 1966 for $800,000. The next day, he gave it to the Christophers in exchange for the one they occupied. Then he sold off that building to a third party. Because of the higher value of the new building, the exchange amounted to a gain by the Christophers of a building worth twice as much as the one they had previously occupied. For Keller, it was the work of many months and many prayers. In addition to having the people he needed to carry on his work, Keller now had the physical structure in which the movement could grow.

* * *

By 1968, Keller began to experience a sharp decline in energy and a slight tremor in his left hand. When he reviewed the tapes of television programs on which he appeared that spring, he knew that his days as a public figure were numbered. It was not just age. Although he did not know it until sometime later, Keller had been stricken with Parkinson's disease, a malady for which there was relief available but no cure.

In a final effort to recover his lost energy, Keller took a long vacation in Ireland as the guest of Albert G. McCarthy, an old friend. Riding by car one day on a trip to Limerick, he realized that his fatigue was not going to go away. He must retire—and soon. He had long planned to step down on his seventieth birthday, June 27, 1970. Instead, he moved up the timetable to early January 1969. He had given the Christophers all that he could. The candle was flickering. In the remaining months of 1968, Keller prepared himself and his staff for his retirement. I was his chosen successor.

This story of James Keller ends where it began—on the high note of a surprise party in which there were many lights and few shadows. But that June day, the culmination of one man's life would not have been so full of warmth and illumination had he not overcome many obstacles along the way.

Others who knew Keller would undoubtedly tell a somewhat different story of this man who had touched their lives. And none of the stories—this one included—would display the full reality of the man, which was known only to himself and to his God. In this respect, he exemplified the uniqueness, even the sacredness, of the human person, which was the wellspring of all that he said and did.

* * *

JUNE 26, 1969—James Keller's face wrinkled into a smile of appreciation when a makeshift chorus of performers trotted onstage to belt out a song written for the occasion. It was sung to the tune of "My Favorite Things," from the play, *The Sound of Music:*

*News Notes and bank notes and
typewriters humming,
Lots of donations as sponsors
keep coming,
Thousands of letters that
each morning brings,
These are a few of
my favorite things.*

*Mail bags and books and
addressographs turning,
Millions of newly lit
candles all burning,
Columns and courses and
gifts without strings,
These are a few of
my favorite things.*

James Keller's concluding remarks form a fitting summary of a life well lived:

Thank you! . . . It's a particular joy for me because each one of you has done a lot to change my life. One of the great blessings of this work has been the people it's been my privilege to meet all through these years.

The years are ticking off one by one and it's a great, deep satisfaction to know each one of you—not as well as I'd like to—and know that you're engaged in the same type of work for the Lord. And that you light candles and don't blow them out.

There are so many things in this dream that have been fantastic. I remember when the Christopher movement was first started, about 1944–45. . . . Why even my best friends told me I was crazy. (They have been telling me ever since.) But for some reason or other the thing has gone and that's due largely, under the Lord, to people like you.

You'll only know when you stand before the Lord all that has been accomplished because of what you've done. Not only those present who are gathered here but some who couldn't be present. It's just beyond words to express to you the consolations which are really a foretaste of heaven.

I am at a loss to tell you how deeply grateful I am to each and all of you for all you have done. I wish that I could list these things but then we'd have a book. But all I can say is: God bless and speed you and thank you.

Epilogue

In January 1970, in a letter to readers of Christopher News Notes, James Keller announced his retirement. He cited "declining health" and characteristically said more about his successor than himself. His letter concluded with a familiar exhortation: "The future of Christopher work knows no bounds. 'You can change the world' is a timeless reminder that each one of us has a unique role to play in bringing the love and truth of the Lord into every phase of human endeavor. . . . God Bless You!"

The announcement was greeted by thousands of letters of appreciation. The famous and the not-so-famous all paid tribute to the man who had, in a variety of ways, led them to become involved in a wider world than they had ever known. But it was the unknown "Christophers" who touched most on the human dimensions of Keller's influence. A woman in Massachusetts wrote:

> My first answer to your "change of command" letter never went out—too emotional. I am sincerely wishing you better health, less stress, more time for writing or reading or resting. You will always be needed. You have been such a wonderful inspiration to thousands. I could bet "your children" created VISTA, Peace Corps, etc. It [your idea] will never die, it will never be all done but it's being done.

A man in California expressed astonishment at the retirement notice. "I have been aware of your fine movement for several years," he wrote, "and as the years go by I have become more convinced that it is one of the finest apostolates that we have today."

A nun in Illinois wrote to thank Keller for his Christian service to the world and to her personally, saying "that much of the openness to the world and emphasis on bringing Christ into the secularization of things and institutions, which was heralded so beautifully in *Gaudium et Spes*,[1] was preceded deeply and simply in the Christopher movement and in you."

A college teacher in Georgia compared Keller's notes to her as being "like a warm encouraging handclasp," which meant more to her than any sermons or psychiatry. Another commented that "you have shown us the way and value of changing ourselves in order to change the world."

The letters were touching in their frankness. "Your letter has saddened me although I can understand and appreciate your position," wrote a woman in Illinois. "I do want you to know, however, what a source of inspiration your work has been to me and countless others. Through the years, I have found guidance, wisdom and motivation in all your writings. I know I am a better person because of you and never will I forget your positive ideas."

A note of hope amid discouragement ran through many letters, as in this note from a realtor in California:

> You have no idea how the news of your retirement affected me. Sure, we all get older, we're all replaced, we'd all like to sit back and take it easy. But somehow, with you, I never thought the day would come. And yet, why not? Why shouldn't you, like the artist, the sculptor, the builder or the craftsman, step back and review the wonders of your work? And what a wonderful and marvelous job you've done! Although we have never met, may I be numbered among the hundreds of thousands who owe you a great debt of gratitude. Your letters and books have helped me. Many a time they kept me going when I felt there really wasn't any point in carrying on.

With his empathy for writers, Keller must have taken satisfaction in this letter from California:

> I first became a writer, of some success, with articles published in several of the national magazines. Remember my delight when I sent the equivalent of my first check to the Christophers? I have worked with Mexican-American families, Negro students,

outpatients at County Hospital, young people in our church, and in many other places. I shall continue to write about human relations with a positive point of view, and keep in mind Christopher and Christian ideals as I deal with my people.

A television program director in Hartford, Connecticut, wrote in wonderment at the longevity of the Christopher program:

It was with mixed emotions that I read of your retirement this past week as it came over our A.P. ticker. . . . THE CHRISTO- PHERS must surely be our longest-running program. I first booked it to begin in 1952 and it is still with us. I can only speculate warmly as to the number of candles it has lit in our area during all these years, as it has done all over the world.

An advertising executive in South Carolina found in Keller's retirement an occasion for writing a long-delayed note:

The periodic News Notes have helped me through the some- times disheartening shadows on the trail of a lay vocation in the marketplace . . . [through] wire service staff days, radio and television news and then advertising sales years, station man- agement, weekly publishing and now the conduct of a slowly thriving regional advertising agency. At this point in your life, I hope that one more grateful report may help bring home how many lives your 'one candle' has brightened. With this help, my one career has reached hundreds of thousands of persons as only the American communications system can do, and each has I hope seen reflected the principles you sought to disseminate.

A publishing executive in Virginia took note of how Keller man- aged to bring forth fresh ideas from the most ancient institution in Christendom: "Your non-sectarian movement in the spirit of Jesus, worked within the framework of the Roman Catholic Church, proves to all who would heed that one need not destroy an institution to create and expedite refreshing new ideas."

And a final tribute from an old Hollywood friend, Robert Young, who said in 1980:

I loved him very dearly. I welcomed every opportunity to help him. With his human and humanistic approach, he was able to

get his personal appeal across to people. He had only to call
and they'd respond. He was a remarkable person. I have adopted
the creed of the Christophers as a personal creed of my own.[2]

* * *

For seven years following his retirement in 1969, Keller maintained an office at Christopher headquarters where he became more
accessible to his own staff and to visitors. His advice was sought
and always received a respectful hearing. The years had mellowed
him. Those who spoke with him came away with a feeling of
warmth mixed with sadness that he was no longer the vigorous
"giant of a man" he had once been described as being.

To his staff, Keller became a no-longer-distant father. To his
fellow Maryknollers, he was now an esteemed brother. To his
Church, a son worthy of some mark of approval. That moment
came on January 21, 1976, when Terence Cardinal Cooke, Archbishop of New York, conferred on Keller the *Benemerenti* medal
blessed by Pope Paul VI. The ceremony, a simple affair, took
place before the entire staff at the Christopher office. Also present
were two Maryknoll bishops, John Comber and Charles Brown,
Father Raymond Hill, the superior general, and a number of
priests. The medal was a sign of papal commendation for Keller's
fifty years in the priesthood, serving Maryknoll and the Christophers.

* * *

Of Keller's role in the Church and world, Avery Dulles, a lifelong friend and a theologian of wide repute, had this to say:

> Keller was a charismatic person in a way unique to himself.
> His special charism was to bring out the best in other people.
> He underplayed his own role and made everybody else feel
> important. . . . He had important insights from the Holy Spirit
> about how to involve the laity in the work of the Church and
> how to bring about collaboration between Catholics and other
> people of good will. There was a tremendous vacuum and he
> singlehandedly went into it. He encouraged apostolic initiative
> on the part of Catholics and others of sound moral principle.
> He set up a network of influential people across the country.
> At that time, it was exactly what the Spirit seemed to be asking
> of the Church. Catholics were isolated. Father Keller brought

a freshness and a novelty of presentation that were important at the time.[3]

Another Jesuit theologian, Alfonso Nebreda, who had been close to Keller said:

> My own recollection is one of profound reverence and affection for the great man that Jim was. His defects or simple limitations have been stressed so often that there is danger to [sic] ignore the fact that he had an uncanny intuitive grasp of the essentials in Christian spirituality . . . . He was so often surprised in his humility when I would simply document his intuitions and show him that, without bookish paraphernalia, he had managed to go to the heart of the Tradition and thus liberate himself from so much dead weight that we younger people had been taught as "traditional" in the pre-Vatican [II] days. I am sure that others must have shown how advanced Jim was in his whole idea of the Christophers, almost a pioneer [who] would rejoice when hearing the pastoral insights of the Council. But I repeat, this was something that obviously he culled from a kind of connaturality with the true sources of the Christian Tradition— and that is, in my view, the connection with his deep spirituality.[4]

* * *

Shortly after he received the papal medal, Keller entered New York Hospital for a periodic checkup on his Parkinsonism. While there, he slipped and broke his hip. Over the next six months, he convalesced at Maryknoll's nursing facility, only to break his other hip in the summer of 1976. The end came on February 7, 1977. Dr. George Cotzias, the world-renowned specialist who supervised Keller's treatment, told the priest in one of their final meetings: "I can thank you for 90 percent of all that I have learned." What the doctor meant by this is open to speculation. What he had learned, perhaps, was how a once-dynamic man came to accept inactivity, infirmity, and the prospect of death in a spirit of uncomplaining faith. Even when he could give nothing else to those around him, James Keller touched them by what Cardinal Newman had called the "slow, silent, penetrating influence of patience." Through this influence, even to the end, James Keller had found one last way to change the world.

Notes

CHAPTER 2
1. The younger priests who accompanied Price to China were Fathers Francis X. Ford, Bernard F. Meyer, and James Edward Walsh.
2. "Educational Policy Change for International Professional Training and Development: A Study of the Maryknoll Fathers, 1912–1978," by Raymond F. Kelly (Ph.D. diss., New York University, 1980).

CHAPTER 3
1. It is hard to keep the Walshes of Maryknoll straight. The cofounder was James Anthony Walsh. James Edward Walsh, the young priest who went to China with Price, became Maryknoll's superior general in 1936.

CHAPTER 4
1. McNicholas, a leading spokesman on national affairs, led the archdiocese from 1925 till his death in 1950. A friend and adviser to Walsh, and therefore to Maryknoll, he espoused the Americanist wing of Catholic thought.

CHAPTER 7
1. Interview with author, September 20, 1980. In a letter dated October 1936, Keller refers to criticisms directed to him by Drought and Byrne, but no written record has been found.
2. Demetrius B. Zema, S.J., in his introduction to *The Thirteenth, the Greatest of Centuries*, by James J. Walsh (New York: AMS Press, 1952).
3. *The Survival of American Innocence* (Notre Dame, Ind.: University of Notre Dame Press, 1980), p. 100.
4. New York: Sheed and Ward, 1963, pp. 9 and 10.
5. New York: Harper, 1952, pp. 217f.

CHAPTER 8

1. "The Failures of Christianity," *Catholic Mind*, July 22, 1941. Keller's copy of this issue was heavily underscored.

2. James Keller's election as a delegate to the Maryknoll Chapter coincided with news of his mother's death. He did not attend the funeral, but several months later he returned home to take care of family matters.

3. Interview with author, August 29, 1980.

CHAPTER 9

1. One of them was shortening the term of office for the Maryknoll General Council from ten years to six. This took place at the 1966 Chapter.

2. A possible reference to Catholic Action.

3. In 1939, largely through Keller's efforts, Maryknoll had acquired a promotion house in the heart of midtown Manhattan at 121 East 39th Street.

4. Letter to author, September 30, 1980.

5. Letter to author, August 28, 1980.

6. Letter to author, August 27, 1980.

7. Letter to author, September 15, 1980.

8. Interview with author, February 12, 1981.

CHAPTER 10

1. Letter to author from Fulton Oursler, Jr., February 15, 1982.

2. Interview with author, September 20, 1980.

3. Communist influence in U.S. unions had crested by this time. By the end of the war, they controlled sixteen international unions, with about 25 percent of the C.I.O. membership. "By [1949] the Communist threat to the labor movement had been largely overcome either through victories of anti-Communists in existing unions or by their desertion to new unions" (Aaron S. Abell, *American Catholicism and Social Action* [Garden City, N.Y.: Doubleday, 1960], p. 278). But the threat from racketeers continued unabated through the 1950s.

4. Critics would note that neither the Constitution nor the Bill of Rights refers explicitly to God, though the origin of human rights may have been implicit.

5. Letter to author, April 1, 1981.

CHAPTER 11

1. *New York Times*, July 18, 1982.

2. The author.

3. *New York Times*, May 4, 1937.

4. *Careers That Change Your World*, by James Keller (New York: Christopher Books, 1950), p. 15.

5. *The C.I.O. and the Communist Party*, by Max Kampelman (New York: Praeger, 1957), p. 153.

6. A Catholic weekly with a circulation of at least 600,000.

7. Gabriel Richard was a nineteenth-century priest who served in the territorial legislature before Michigan became a state.

8. Letter to author, March 30, 1982.

9. Keller was a laborious rewriter. He estimated that he revised the introductory chapter of *You Can Change the World* thirty-one times.

CHAPTER 12

1. In 1936, the Maryknoll General Chapter petitioned the Holy See for permission to begin missions among the Negroes in the southern United States. Rome replied in the negative.

CHAPTER 13

1. With $30,000 for book awards and $10,000 for drama awards, the Christopher impact was considerable.

CHAPTER 14

1. Interview with author, September 1980.

2. Interview with author, September 1980.

3. Murray was opposed to further atomic testing and to larger atomic bombs. He favored government, rather than private, production of atomic energy. In addition, Murray sought unsuccessfully to give the public greater access to information on the dangers as well as the positive aspects of the atom. He was one of the first to inform the public of the dangers of Strontium 90 and called for recognition of the "forgotten equation" linking morality with national defense. Murray frequently clashed with Lewis L. Strauss, head of the A.E.C.

CHAPTER 15

1. Transcript of interview on "Christopher Closeup."

CHAPTER 16

1. Interview with author, September 1980.

2. Interview with author, September 1980.

3. The priest was Father Paul Anderson, later to become bishop of Duluth, Minnesota.

4. Interview with author, September 1980.

CHAPTER 18

1. Letter to author, October 31, 1980.

CHAPTER 19

1. John Newington, a wealthy investor, began supporting the Christophers in 1947. In the mid-fifties, he invited Keller to make his weekend home with him and his wife.

2. Letter to author, October 1980.

3. Myles Bourke, St. Joseph's Seminary, N.Y.; James Connelly, Bishop Dubois High School, N.Y.; Bernard Cooke, S.J., Marquette University; P. Damboriena; Georges Delcuve, S.J., *Lumen Vitae* Institute, Brussels; Avery Dulles, S.J., Woodstock College, Maryland; Peter Fransen, S.J., Louvain and Innsbruck; Joseph Grassi, M.M., Maryknoll Seminary; Jerome Hamer, O.P., Assistant General, Dominicans, Roman; Bernard Häring, C.SS.R., Alfonsianum Institute, Rome; Ronan Hoffman, O.F.M., Conv., Catholic University, Washington; Edward Malone, M.M., Maryknoll Seminary; Alfonso Nebreda, S.J., Sophia University, Tokyo; Frank Norris, S.S., St. Patrick's Seminary, Menlo Park, Calif.; Maurice Queguiner, M.E.P., Superior General, Paris Foreign Missions; Shawn Sheehan, St. John's Seminary, Brighton, Mass.; Gerard Sloyan, Catholic University, Washington, D.C.; Theodore Stone, Assistant Director, CCD, Chicago; Edmund Veillesse, C.I.C.M., Scheut Seminary, Belgium; and Eugene Walsh, S.S., St. Mary's Seminary, Baltimore.

4. Vol. 26 (1965), pp. 486–490.

5. Rev. John Frauenfelder, interview with author, October 1981.

6. Mrs. Rita Cushman, letter to author, July 11, 1981.

7. Letter to author June 29, 1982.

CHAPTER 20

1. John Considine had been loaned to the U.S. bishops a few years earlier to set up the Latin America Bureau in Washington.

2. Letter to author, April 27, 1982.

EPILOGUE

1. Latin title of the Second Vatican Council's Constitution on the Church in the Modern World.

2. Telephone conversation with author, September 1980.

3. Interview with author, September 1980.

4. Letter to author, March 20, 1982.

Index